HOW TO ...

support students with Autism Spectrum Condition in secondary school

Lynn McCann

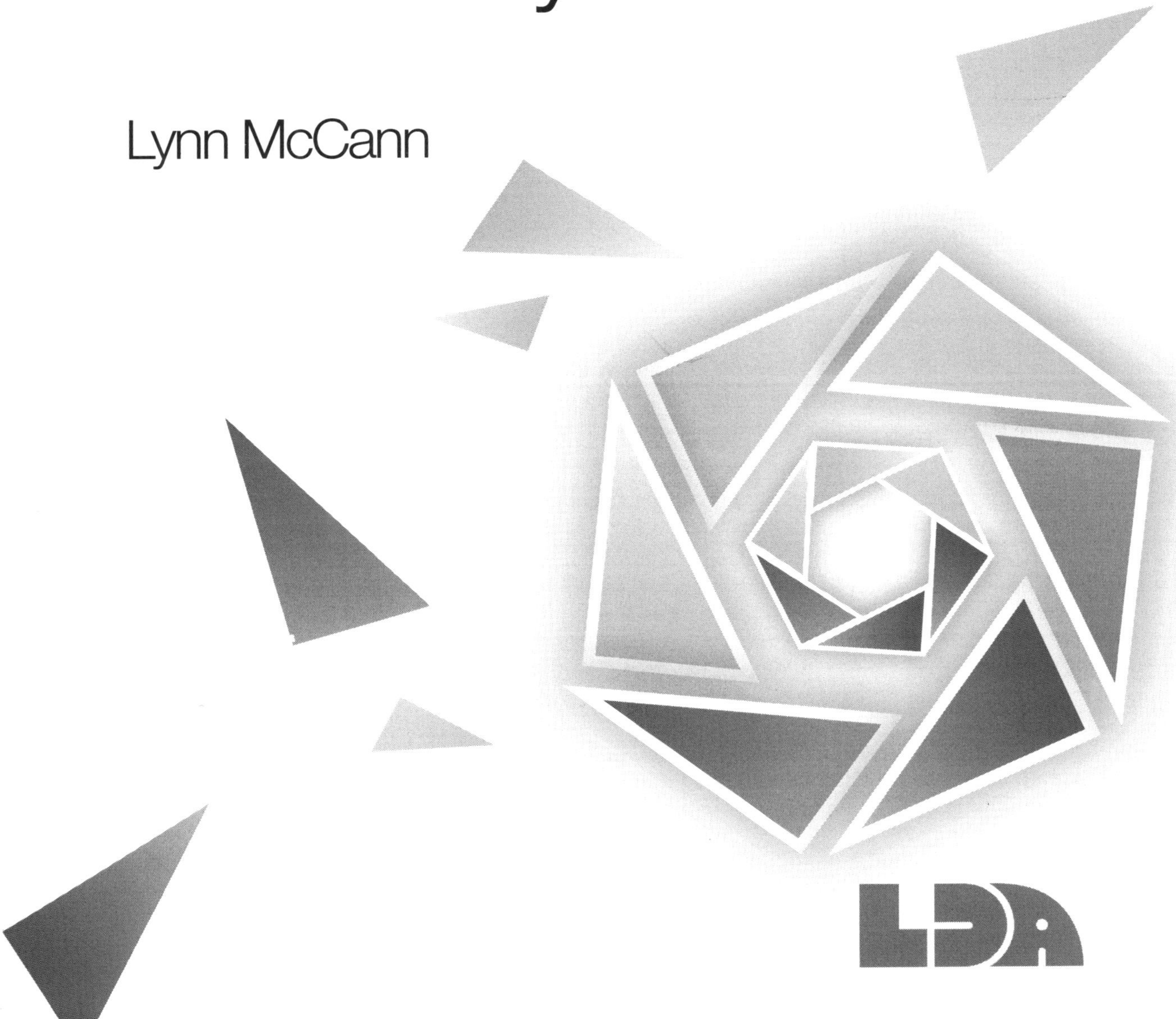

LDA

Acknowledgements

I would like to thank all the SENCOs, teaching staff and parents that I have worked with over the past ten years, in special, primary and secondary schools. You have all taught me so much, you have worked so hard and together we've seen so many children and young people overcome challenges and thrive in school.

To the children who are autistic, thank you. You are talented, interesting, unique and a joy to work with. I hope this book helps your teachers support you well and that you go on to be the best person that you could ever be.

To my husband Steve and my children Siobhan and Matthew, I love you and thank you for allowing me the space and time to write my books.

How to support students with Autism Spectrum Condition in secondary school

ISBN: 978-1-85503-603-1

© Lynn McCann 2017
Illustrations by Robin Lawrie

This edition published 2017
10 9 8 7 6

Printed in the UK by Page Bros (Norwich) Ltd
Designed and typeset by Andy Wilson for Green Desert Ltd

LDA, 2 Gregory Street, Hyde, Cheshire, SK14 4HR

www.ldalearning.com

The right of Lynn McCann to be identified as the author of this work has been asserted in accordance with Sections 77 and 78 of the Copyright, Designs and Patents Act 1988.

All rights reserved. This book contains materials which may be reproduced by photocopier or other means for use by the purchaser. The permission is granted on the understanding that these copies will be used within the educational establishment of the purchaser. The book and all its contents remain copyright. Copies may be made without reference to the publisher or the licensing scheme for the making of photocopies operated by the Publishers Licensing Society.

CONTENTS

	Preface	v
1	What is Autism Spectrum Condition?	1
2	Transition into secondary school	11
3	Accessing classwork	17
4	Advice for subject teachers	25
5	Homework	41
6	Social communication and interaction	49
7	Tests and examinations	60
8	Supporting behaviour	63
9	Managing emotions	75
10	Sensory regulation	84
11	Bullying	88
12	Sex and relationships	97
13	Transition between Key Stages 3–4 and 4–5	103
14	Conclusion	107
	References	110
	Further resources Useful websites	112

CD-ROM contents

Student passport template
Checklist for the early weeks of secondary school
Homework support plan template
Social skills checklist for ASC students
My steps to success
Social detective
I can do a test! social story
Rules
Student behaviour questionnaire
STAR record template
Emotion words chart template
Body-mapping template
Emotion-mapping template
Problem-solving map
Transition map

All websites were correct at the time of going to print.

PREFACE

I have counselled, supported, taught and observed hundreds of secondary students with Autism Spectrum Conditions (ASC) and watched with awe as Year 7s turn into Year 11s and prepare for the step into further education. They grow and change in so many ways: physically, emotionally and academically, and there are so many challenges for the student during their secondary years that knowledgeable and skilled staff are needed to listen to and support them. Students with ASC may be different at times, but being accepted and included are as important to them as any student.

This book is for SENCOs, teachers, teaching assistants (TAs), learning support assistants (LSAs) and senior managers. It is intended to be used as a reference throughout the time the student with ASC is in your school or class. It will help you understand the student's condition and support their strengths and differences. From key skill support in each subject to social inclusion, mental health and puberty, every student with ASC will need a support plan that will be cohesive across their whole school experience. This will need someone, usually the SENCO, to make sure subject teachers know the essential information about the student, and who monitors their progress and is able to identify any issues early enough for them not to become crisis. We discuss behaviour, sanctions, homework and testing so that each teacher can understand the value of consistency and have strategies that they can use to support the student with ASC.

> *I hope that you learn that every student is individual and the key is to understand them and their autism, because the way ASC 'works' in each student is unique.*

Learning and discovering together is part of the joy of the ASC journey. Let the student be your guide as you build a relationship of trust, and learn how to communicate with each other.

Please note that while every effort has been made to use inclusive language, the term 'parent' has been used for the sake of brevity in many cases, but can also refer to a young person's carer.

CHAPTER 1
What is Autism Spectrum Condition?

The term Autism Spectrum Condition (ASC) has had a number of labels over the years. It encompasses the labels Asperger's syndrome and autism. Many professionals and authorities use the term Autism Spectrum Disorder (ASD), but more and more professionals (like the eminent autism researcher Simon Baron-Cohen) are adopting the term 'condition' rather than 'disorder'.

We are now learning that autism is a difference in the way the brain processes experiences, information and sensory stimulation, and there are strengths and talents associated with this. Therefore, it seems proper that we see it as a 'condition' rather than a 'disorder'. This is important, given that over 1% of our population is now thought to have an ASC (The National Autistic Society, 2012). Whereas some people with an ASC have associated learning disabilities and co-existing conditions, many are able to achieve academically and in life. With the right support, employment and family life can be as accessible to people with ASC as the general population.

> **'Autistic students' or 'students with ASC'?**
>
> *There is a lot of debate amongst the autism community and within professional circles about whether to use person-first or personal terms for someone who is on the autistic spectrum. Whereas many adults with the condition seem to prefer the term 'autistic' as it defines who they are, many professionals continue to use person-first language. This book will use the term 'students with ASC', whilst recognising the preference that some may have to be spoken of as 'autistic'. It is recommended that any SENCO or teacher asks the student and their parents or carers to identify which term they prefer.*

ASC is considered to be a condition that a person is born with and will have all their lives. It is generally accepted that it is a difference in the way the brain is 'wired' and is part of human neurodiversity. A person with ASC can have difficulties or differences in communicating and understanding communication with people around them, socialising and understanding the complexity of social information. They may have strong and sometimes rigid thinking patterns, find guessing what others might think difficult and have differences in the way their senses experience the world. They may also have strong emotional responses and differences in the way they process emotions.

As a spectrum condition, every person with ASC, although having been diagnosed within the parameters of the condition, will present a unique set of lifelong strengths and challenges.

Therefore, a young person with ASC will become an adult with ASC, and is a person with infinite capabilities. Young people who had speech and language difficulties from a young age have the ability to continue learning and developing their skills and can go on to achieve well in their adult lives.

Too often we focus on a student's difficulties and label the student as disruptive or unable to achieve. *This is not true.* All students with ASC are capable of making progress and achieving success if the right understanding, support and expectations are in place for them by the teachers and TAs that they meet each year in school.

Diagnosis

There are currently two sets of criteria that are used in the UK for the diagnosis of ASC. These are contained in the *International Statistical Classification of Diseases and Related Health Problems* (World Health Organisation, 2016) and the American *Diagnostic and Statistical Manual of Mental Disorders* (American Psychiatric Association, 2015). These documents identity the characteristics of autism as being marked differences and impairments in social communication and interaction, with restricted interests and rigid and repetitive behaviours. Recently the criteria in the *Diagnostic and Statistical Manual of Mental Disorders (DSM-5™)* has been reviewed to include the area of sensory processing, which is an important change. According to the *DSM-5™* two areas have been categorised for diagnosis with additional considerations as stated:

Revised diagnostic criteria for Autism Spectrum Disorder in the *DSM-5*™

- **A** Persistent deficits in social communication and social interaction across multiple contexts, as manifested by the following, currently or by history:
  1. Deficits in social-emotional reciprocity
  2. Deficits in non-verbal communicative behaviours used for social interaction
  3. Deficits in developing, maintaining and understanding relationships.

- **B** Restricted, repetitive patterns of behaviour, interests or activities as manifested by at least two of the following, currently or by history:
  1. Stereotyped or repetitive motor movements, use of objects, or speech
  2. Insistence on sameness, inflexible adherence to routines, or ritualised patterns of verbal or non-verbal behaviour
  3. Highly restricted, fixated interests that are abnormal in intensity or focus
  4. Hyper- or hypo-reactivity to sensory input or unusual interest in sensory aspects of the environment.

- **C** Symptoms must be present in the early developmental period (but may not become fully manifest until social demands exceed limited capacities, or may be masked by learned strategies in later life).

- **D** Symptoms cause clinically significant impairment in social, occupational or other important areas of current functioning.

- **E** These disturbances are not better explained by intellectual disability (intellectual developmental disorder), or global developmental delay.

(www.dsm5.org, 2016)

Looking at the world from an autistic viewpoint

To help teaching staff understand how ASC affects how students experience everything in their lives it is valuable to look at the following areas in more detail through the perspective of young people with ASC, and consider the stresses and demands that they may experience every day.

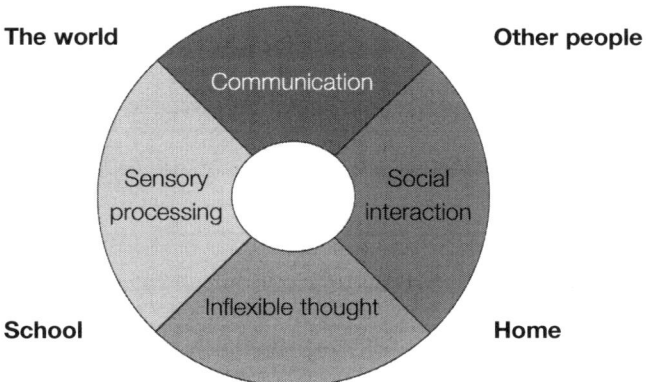

Fig. 1: Autism affects every part of a student's life.

Communication

The communication skills of students with ASC vary widely. Some will have had delayed language development as young children and may have received speech therapy in their early years and maybe throughout primary school, whereas others will have had almost precocious speech that included complex vocabulary and the ability to memorise large chunks of dialogue. However, what is common in all students with ASC is the difficulty in using their spoken language to understand, process and create language quickly enough for the demands of the situation.

> Often students with ASC can understand language literally. Therefore, everything that is said is understood without taking into account any inference, implied meaning, context or sarcasm. For these students, idioms and metaphors can be very confusing.

Taking the bull by the horns.

Being able to 'read' non-verbal communication may be difficult and impact on their understanding of the spoken words. In school, the ability to turn what they know into coherent written communication can be very difficult for some students with ASC, especially if it is imaginative, abstract, requires them to explain different opinions or is something in which they have no interest.

Not understanding how we use inference and tone of voice to emphasise meaning can result in the student with ASC missing a lot of the communication in class and around school.

Social interaction

Every situation throughout the student's day demands communication with others, from interactions with their family in the morning, travelling to and walking into school, trying to find familiar people amongst a lot of unfamiliar faces in the outside area, different classrooms and teachers, sudden changes of personnel, break times and lunchtimes, then finally home time, maybe a trip to the shop or going out with parents.

Generally, young people develop social skills through some instruction but also through an enormous capacity to assimilate what they see others doing into their own behaviour. A lot of this development happens naturally, but students with ASC can have very uneven social development due to them lacking in the important social skills needed to interact with different groups of people such as:

Eye contact

Some have difficulty using eye contact which means that they miss the connection with other people that communicates shared attention, trust and non-verbal communication. Some students with ASC may even have **face-blindness** which means recognising even their close associates may be difficult. Others may use peripheral vision to limit the intense overload their brain receives from looking directly at a person or situation. They are able to see what is around them without the pain and discomfort caused by looking at something directly, but then can be accused of not paying attention.

Non-verbal communication

It is common in students with ASC to have little ability to 'read' a person's non-verbal communication; facial expressions, body language, gestures and posture can all seem threatening and confusing or, for some, make no sense at all. However some, including girls with ASC, can over-read facial expressions, body language and other non-verbal cues which can make them very anxious around others, and be in constant fear of upsetting people or getting something wrong.

Hypersensitivity

Some people with ASC are hypersensitive to other people's facial expressions and moods, to a point that they 'feel' too strongly when they are around others and can seem very anxious, withdrawn or unable to communicate effectively in small or large groups.

Conversation

Understanding the social conventions and 'rules' of conversations may be difficult to grasp. Some students with ASC may cope by dominating conversations, insisting on talking about their special interest every time, or seem to constantly interrupt. Others may be withdrawn, very quiet and feel very anxious when a contribution to a conversation is demanded of them.

Difficulties making and keeping friends

Most students with ASC do want to have friends. However, they want friends who have the same interests as them and will make them feel comfortable. Loyalty is very important as the student with ASC may not have the skills to repair communication breakdowns. The complexities of friendships may be quite overwhelming for students with ASC and they may easily become left without friends or vulnerable to teasing and bullying. The added dimension of social media during the secondary school years often only adds to their distress.

Inflexible thought

Research using MRI brain scans shows that the autistic brain may be 'wired' differently to a neurotypical brain. This can mean that certain skills are more efficient in the autistic brain, such as seeing patterns, systemising, being an expert in one area of interest or visual processing, whereas other skills can be much less efficiently processed, such as social communication and understanding, predicting social outcomes, planning, self-organising, self-monitoring, emotional communication and imagining what a situation might be like. This is related to a part of the brain which deals with **executive functioning** (Wertz, 2012). Executive functioning is the thinking skills that help the brain organise and act on information. These skills enable students to plan, organise, remember things, prioritise, self-monitor, pay attention and know how to start activities. Being able to use information and experiences from the past to solve current problems is an executive function too. These skills are often quite poor in people with autism, even into adulthood. This has a number of effects on the student in daily and school life. These include:

Anxiety about change

Difficulty in predicting what something will be like can mean the student with ASC is resistant to, and very anxious about, change. Sometimes even small changes – such as not using their usual pen or sitting in a different place – can cause extreme anxiety. Often changes in school such as a substitute teacher, a timetable change, their TA being seconded to another activity, an off-timetable day, outside visits, etc. are not communicated well to the student and cause extreme anxiety, withdrawal or meltdowns.

Self-organisation

Many students with ASC find it difficult to organise themselves, which impacts on their ability to get ready for a lesson, tidy up, get changed for PE and gather all the things they need for home time. Poor executive functioning can also affect the ability to even start a piece of work independently; the brain cannot move on to the work without some kind of prompt or support to get started. In some students with ASC this is quite severe and a lot of prompting and support is needed to do every piece of work.

Understanding points of view

One of the common difficulties for students with ASC is in understanding different points of view and the perspectives of a situation that might be different from theirs. This rigidity of thinking can cause them difficulty in the curriculum, in getting along with others and in interpreting incidents that happen around school. They may also become fixated on an issue or event that they feel very strongly about and can find it difficult to move on or stop thinking about it. Again, some may become very anxious as they do understand that there are different points of view but may not be able to draw all the views into a coherent and overall understanding.

Memory and recall

Some students with ASC find it difficult to organise and recall things in their memory. They may be able to recall lots of facts and information about their own interests but cannot recall what they did in your lesson only yesterday. This may be linked to a poor concept of time (in that we store events in time order in our memory) and knowing where to find the information in their jumbled memory, which can take too long to process in the time they have. Sensory processing is the brain's ability to organise and regulate the sensory systems. All the information we take in from and about the world around us comes in through our senses and dictates how we respond to changes in our own body, the environment and how we interact or respond to the situations and people we come into contact with.

Motivation and self-esteem

Students with ASC may show poor motivation when faced with subjects and activities they are not interested in, don't understand, think they cannot do, or do not know the outcome of.

Some students with ASC can refuse to do work because they believe they will fail. It may be writing a story, doing a maths test or an art project. They may have had some difficulty with the task or subject in the past, or it is something new that they do not understand, and so are so overwhelmed with anxiety that refusing to do the work seems more logical to them than trying to do it.

This is where we can use their interests to great effect. Strong special interests bring pleasure and feelings of success to a student with ASC and help to build up their self-esteem and success in areas they may not find easy by linking their learning to their interests. Ultimately, they are more likely to seek a career connected to their interests than in a subject they are struggling to understand.

Sensory processing

Having a Sensory Processing Disorder (SPD) impacts on the person's daily experiences at home, school and out in the community, making it difficult for them to 'filter' or 'switch off' from sensory overload. Some may find that they get great pleasure from certain sensory experiences and will crave the joy that engaging in spinning, jumping or twisting something might bring them. Others may seek out smells, tastes or want to touch and fiddle with everything. Conversely, some people with SPD find the world far too loud, smelly and overwhelming, leading to much anxiety and distress. Having heightened sensations can be exhausting when you can see, hear, smell, taste or feel *everything* all at once. Many students with ASC have SPD as part of their condition (hence its inclusion in the diagnostic criteria) but it can also be part of Attention Deficit Hyperactivity Disorder (ADHD), Down's syndrome or not connected to another condition at all (see more in Chapter 10).

ASC and puberty

Students with ASC will face different challenges as they go through the stages of puberty. As with all students they are developing and changing from a child to an adult and the way their ASC affects them will develop too. It is therefore important to continue to assess and seek understanding of the student's condition throughout their secondary school years and change and adapt strategies and support as necessary. As they move into Key Stage 4 this will include transition to post-16 study, or work, but also should include time to understand who they are and how their diagnosis affects them (see Chapter 13 for more information about supporting students with ASC through this time).

Strengths of ASC

Having an autistic brain may have certain strengths and advantages. Common strengths are related to the preferences a student with ASC may have for:

- **Observing things in fine detail.** The ability to see fine detail and remember things that seem unimportant to others can support artistic or musical ability, mathematical knowledge, scientific or other subject expertise and excellent report writing.
- **Logical reasoning.** Thinking about a problem logically can be a very useful strength in all areas of the curriculum and in life. When others may be blinded by emotional responses, a student with autism may be able to state the logical and truthful

observation or answer. We can harness this in the classroom and support the student with ASC to bring their logical reasoning to a group problem-solving activity. It will be important to listen to them and make them feel that their contribution is valuable but also teach them that others may have different ideas and opinions and that it is okay for them to do so.

- **Adherence to rules.** This can mean that the student is eager to get things right and complete a task to fulfil the rules. However, this may also lead to some considerable anxiety which students will need support in place for.
- **Honesty and loyalty.** Honesty may sometimes not be what others want to hear but we can support this by teaching others to appreciate and not take things too personally. Supporting friendships in the early days will be important so that they can grow and become established. With support, this can result in lifelong friendships.
- **Visual thinking.** If visual strategies are used for those who are visual thinkers, then their ability to learn and think about a task can be greatly enhanced. However, it is important to check each student's learning strengths and not to assume that all students with ASC are visual learners.
- **Computer skills.** Many students with ASC are very gifted in using computers and their skills should be channelled into supporting their school work appropriately.
- **Sense of humour.** There are a number of comedians with ASC (e.g. the famous comedian and actor, Dan Ackroyd). Getting to know a student's sense of humour can be one of the most rewarding ways of interacting with them.
- **Special interests and expertise.** Many students with ASC have special interests and vast knowledge about particular topics of interest. They are at their most engaging and interesting when talking about their special interests. Their interests and expertise should lead to their careers where possible.

As with any other individual, students with ASC have their own personalities and life experiences and should be encouraged to identify and make the best of their talents and skills. Developing their area of expertise and being given the opportunity to coach and support others can develop a caring role and their empathetic nature.

Some students with ASC can be great advocates for ASC awareness and support within schools. They can talk about their condition to help others understand and promote tolerance and inclusion, as well as get involved in charity support and promotion to support the school's inclusion ethos.

Girls with ASC

Up until very recently it was believed that there were far more boys than girls with autism. However, research is now showing us that there are far more girls on the autistic spectrum than was previously thought. This is due in part to autism presenting differently in girls, and to the assumption that girls do not have autism as regularly as boys, resulting in many girls on the autistic spectrum being misdiagnosed or remaining undiagnosed. The National Autistic Society and the Lorna Wing Research Centre have been studying the difference between how autism might affect females and have concluded that many females may be undiagnosed because of these differences (Gould & Ashton-Smith, 2011).

If you think a girl in your school may be on the autism spectrum, seek advice from an autism specialist teacher or an educational psychologist, who will be able to guide you and parents through the process of diagnosis. Here are some of the features to look out for in girls:

Communication

Boys with ASC are often identified by their behaviour – when they cannot find the words to use, they use actions to make their needs known. Whilst girls on the spectrum can sometimes do this, often they can be more passive. They may internalise their distress and be more vulnerable to mental health issues. They may be withdrawn or 'moody' or just ignore the demands, rather than challenge them.

Girls with ASC may speak in a babyish tone or have no regard for the hierarchy of authority in school so can be seen as cheeky or rude, when they are just stating facts. Girls, like boys, often take language literally and so misunderstanding and confusion prevents them really 'getting' what is going on around them or what the teacher really means. Conversely, they can also be extremely articulate and able in certain subjects.

If a girl on the autistic spectrum gets along by imitating the social behaviours of those around her, she may not be able to discriminate which behaviours are appropriate and which are not.

Social interaction

Girls on the autistic spectrum can seem more socially active, but they can want to dominate and be in control of the friendship group or cope by imitating the social behaviour of a group. Often they cannot cope with jokes, teasing and communication breakdowns. They may throw a tantrum or withdraw when things are difficult for them. On the other hand, they may seem the life and soul of the group but struggle to maintain the friendships beyond a basic level. Conversely, they may not be able to cope with the complexities of teenage social relationships and be completely left out of any social groups. They can be highly anxious and withdrawn, seemingly wanting to be on their own, and be on the receiving end of cruel jibes and bullying by other girls. They may be so quiet and seeking to avoid notice that you are hardly aware of them.

Girls on the autistic spectrum can 'feel' intensely. One feeling can be that of intense shame when they don't get something right, especially socially. They often cannot tell the difference between a small social mistake – something that everyone else would just brush off and move on from – or a big mistake that marks you out as odd. Consequently, a lot of stress and awkwardness can be felt when they are in any classroom groups or social situations.

Inflexible thought

To an onlooker, the play of girls with ASC can seem very imaginative and girls on the spectrum can lose themselves intensely in books and characters. The play, however, is very strict and controlled (e.g. a doll is called a name, given a character and nothing can change that identity once it has been assigned). The special interests the girl has can be seemingly usual interests for girls, such as ponies or celebrities, but they can become very intense and all-consuming and younger interests can still be present in the secondary years, when their peers are moving onto adolescent interests. This is often when girls with ASC are noticed as possibly having ASC.

Girls with ASC can have the same difficulties with lack of organisation and planning as boys on the spectrum do. They may have also become obsessive organisers who need to control everything or they become very distressed. Change and new situations will also be difficult and girls can be as likely as boys to exhibit characteristics of Pathological Demand Avoidance (PDA).

Sensory processing

Sensory issues and dealing with a busy, noisy, smelly, confusing world can be the most stressful thing that a girl with ASC has to deal with. She may be experiencing the world intensely and we need to look for evidence of sensory-seeking or avoiding behaviours, as well as asking her what she can tell us about her world.

Remember that while it is currently not as common as in boys, girls can still have ASC. The features that cause them difficulty can be more evident in the secondary years as the social complexities and relationships around them develop rapidly and can leave them behind. Dealing with friendships, gossip, teasing, emotional awareness, social media and self-image can expose the autism more in girls than in boys, due to the nature of the relationships girls and boys develop in these years. Girls may find themselves excluded from parties, bullied and vulnerable to depression just as much as boys with ASC can be and we should be aware that girls in our schools will need support for their ASC too.

Remember that girls on the autistic spectrum can be fun, talented and clever, and have lots of potential to make a great contribution to the world ... just like the boys!

Co-existing conditions

It is not uncommon for a student with ASC to have been diagnosed with additional conditions. Sometimes ADHD, dyslexia, Developmental Co-ordination Disorder (DCD), dyspraxia, PDA, Obsessive Compulsive Disorder (OCD), Tourette's syndrome or other conditions may have been recorded as a multi-diagnosis. It is important in these situations that staff know about the other conditions and build the strategies that are recommended to support those conditions into your approach, along with the ASC strategies. You will often find that the strategies will complement each other and can work well alongside the usual classroom practice if they are planned and used consistently.

Pathological Demand Avoidance (PDA)

PDA is seen as part of the autism spectrum and is increasingly being recognised by clinicians and therefore children are being given a diagnosis of PDA along with their ASC. However, it remains a controversial condition, not part of the official diagnostic manual (*Diagnostic and Statistical Manual of Mental Disorders*) and isn't recognised by all clinicians. PDA is characterised by extreme anxiety and manipulation to avoid everyday demands. It is almost like having a panic attack whenever the person perceives there may be a demand made upon them. This can include the everyday demands of getting out of bed and getting ready for school, someone saying their name, and getting through the routines of the day. This high anxiety leaves the person in a constant state of 'fight or flight' and extra demands given by the teacher in order to complete a piece of work, or a parent to carry out an extra small task, such as '*Pick up your socks*', can bring on the panic attack. Some may seem to be in a constant state of meltdown and exhibit challenging behaviours in order to avoid doing the activity demanded of them; others may cope by micro-managing their lives in rituals, routines and manipulating others to try and minimise their anxiety. Children who are suspected of having PDA are often more socially-able than typical ASC students and need a lot of specialised support to enable them to cope with their fear of demands at home and school. PDA in the secondary school can be difficult to manage if it is severe.

If you have a student with a diagnosis of PDA you will need to consider the strategies that you use with caution. Some of the strategies suggested in this book will work well with students with PDA and some will not. For example, demands with choices that give them some control over what they do, work well. The PDA Society (www.pdasociety.org.uk) is a good resource for PDA-specific strategies, which generally include flexible choices and negotiation.

CHAPTER 2
Transition into secondary school

Transition – the moving from one situation to another – can be very difficult for students with ASC as it involves a lot of change and unknown factors. Even daily transitions from classroom to classroom, between different teachers and subjects, and from home to school can take an enormous amount of energy and effort to manage for the student with ASC. This chapter will deal with supporting the major transition from primary into secondary school and once they are there, coping with the numerous daily transitions.

Planning and preparation can make all the difference when a student is facing a transition, and successful transitions are possible.

> *One basic principle is to remember to explain what will be the same, building on what they know and what they are familiar with, as well as outline the new things that they will experience.*

Often when we are preparing for change we will comfort ourselves with working out what will be similar and what new things we can look forward to. Students with ASC need to be able to do this too. If we only focus on the differences we create more anxiety.

A student with ASC in primary school has often had the same teacher and possibly the same support person every day for at least the whole of Year 6. The primary staff will know them well and hopefully will have well-established strategies and resources in place to support the student (although this is not always the case). Every student is different, and some need to keep the same strategies and resources to go with them to secondary school, whereas some will be ready to try new ways of doing things as long as they have been explained clearly to them.

A student who has an Education, Health and Care (EHC) Plan will have paperwork to support this, including records of strategies and resources used. There may be many years of paperwork which the primary school is eager to pass on. The secondary school SENCO is usually responsible for collecting this paperwork and extracting the relevant information to pass on to the subject teachers. It is important to remember that every student with ASC is different, and the best place to begin to assess their support needs will be at a transition meeting, usually held at the primary school. It is important that parents are able to attend this meeting and the secondary SENCO can begin to take responsibility for the student's transition to their school. It is at this meeting that the secondary SENCO can meet the student, gather the information about their needs and form a plan of transition for them.

Difficulty can arise in deciding relevant and helpful information that needs to be passed on to the subject teachers. Many schools have found that a 'Student Passport' document can be easy to read and remember and enables teaching staff to understand the student's needs and the main strategies that they can employ in their subjects.

A Student Passport should:

- contain the student's details (name, date of birth, primary school)
- have a description of the student, preferably written by themselves as well as contributed to by the teaching staff
- be positive
- give a short description to explain their condition and how it affects them. With ASC it is good to explain it in the four areas: communication, social interaction, thinking and sensory processing.
- suggest where they might sit in class and what sensory distractions might occur
- emphasise the student's strengths and interests
- explain how the student learns best and what strategies really help
- include any medical needs and mention if the student has regular medication
- say who the student's friends are and how to support them making new friends
- explain what makes the student anxious and how they can be helped
- include their academic profile, what support and differentiation is needed and how to help them organise their work
- include the professionals that support the student, what their role is and if subject teachers will receive advice from them.

(See page 13 for an example of a completed Student Passport. **For a template for a Student Passport see the CD-ROM.**)

A Student Passport needs to be updated, preferably with the student, at least every year.

When a student has ASC, a successful transition from primary to secondary school starts as early as Year 5. The preparation done by the primary school can prepare the student in partnership with the secondary school.

Many secondary schools have good links and transition planning for all their prospective Year 7s. However, there are additional considerations for students with ASC, for example:

- the student with ASC may be vulnerable to believing or misunderstanding everything other and older students say about secondary school. They can be very literal in their understanding and so tales of 'flushing heads in toilets' can be believed absolutely.
- primary teachers may not know much about secondary school and may be over-anxious for the student
- parents may be very anxious, especially if they have not been inside a secondary school since they were students. They will be aware of, and may be focused on, negative issues such as teasing, bullying, different teachers, homework, travelling to school and detentions.

Student passport: Kirsty Smith

My birthday is 3rd June and I am in Year 7.

My tutor is Mr Hatfield.

I have a diagnosis of Asperger's syndrome and an EHC Plan which gives me extra help in school.

Asperger's is a lifelong condition which affects how a person communicates, interacts socially and can present difficulties or differences for the person in their thinking, imagination, perception and sensitivity of their senses. It affects me in four areas:

Communication – I talk a lot. I love big words and telling people about my interests. But it can be difficult for me to listen and understand all that you mean. I can't organise my thoughts to compose a piece of writing very well.	**Social interaction** – I find it hard to make friends because my Aspergers makes me feel shy and always say the wrong things. One girl who I get on with is Emma from my primary school. I would love to make new friends.
Thinking – I like routines because they make me feel safe. Change makes me feel very anxious. I find it hard to understand other people's points of view – it makes no sense to me.	**Sensory** – loud noises, strong smells, crowded places and people touching me are horrible. They make me feel scared and want to run away.

My strengths and interests

- I love computers, especially Minecraft.
- Reading fantasy novels.
- My dog – Rover.
- I am good at maths.
- I go to a girls with Aspergers support group every month.

I don't like

- Writing. It is really hard for me to think and write.
- Doing PE. I hate the changing rooms.
- Smells.
- Crowds.
- Being touched.
- Loud noises.
- Boys.
- Harry Potter.

Things I find difficult

- Listening to and remembering all the instructions.
- Writing.
- Understanding jokes and teasing.
- Noisy and busy places or activities.
- Working in groups.
- Making friends.
- Getting changed for PE quickly.
- Going on school trips.

How to help me

- Tell me what I need to do using the words *First/Then/Finally*.
- Write down exactly what I have to do in steps.
- Ask me to tell you what I have to do and make sure I have got it right.
- Write down my homework for me.
- Let me work with Emma or another girl as a partner instead of doing group work.
- Let me sit in a place I choose, so I am near the door.
- If I am distressed, let me use my 'time out' card to go out for 5 minutes. Then I will come back in.
- Try not to let the class get too noisy.
- Allow me to go out of class for 2 minutes before the bell to get to my next lesson before the crowds.
- Praise me and help me make friends.
- I like to please my teachers. I like to do jobs at break times too.

Please be aware of my vulnerability to being bullied. Please report distress or incidents to the SENCO.

Fig. 2: An example of a completed Student Passport.

What can help?

The secondary school SENCO usually becomes involved once the student has been allocated a place or before, if they have an EHC Plan. However, if a student does not have an EHC Plan it will be just as important for the secondary school to gather a profile of information about the student's needs once they have been informed that they have an ASC diagnosis. The secondary school may already have a good transition process that includes interactive websites, transition booklets, taster days and even summer schools, but there are additional ideas that can support students with ASC.

- Enable the student to meet key people from the secondary school (e.g. the SENCO) either at their primary school or during extra visits before the main taster day.
- Make arrangement for the student to visit at different times:
    1. when the school is quiet and students are in lessons
    2. when they can see the dining hall, lunchtime and maybe a lunchtime club
    3. at a busier time when they can observe and experience the movement around the school.
- Give the student a camera or video camera to take photos of key places (toilets, reception, learning support, changing rooms, dinner hall, etc.). They can put these in a folder or PowerPoint presentation to look at during the summer break. The student with ASC could make a presentation for the other children at their primary school.
- Arrange for students with ASC in Year 8 who have made a successful transition to talk to the new students and parents to share what has helped them.
- Give the student a school map, timetable and planner to familiarise themselves with before they come to the school. Colour-code areas of the school on the map.
- Create an ASC student transition guide or make adjustments to the existing school guide (such as the *Transition Toolkit* produced by the Autism Education Trust). Include 'what to do if....' as a set of cards that are easily accessible to the student (see page 15).

If I am lost

I can look at my timetable to see the room number.

I can get out my map to see where the room is.

I can ask a teacher or student where the room is.

I can go to reception and ask the secretary where my room is.

If I am late

I need to go to the school office and tell the receptionist that I have arrived.

I will go to my form room or my lesson and tell my teacher I am sorry that I am late.

My teacher will say 'okay' and I can sit in my seat to get on with the lesson.

If I forget my homework

I should tell my teaching assistant as soon as I get to school or realise I have forgotten it.

My teaching assistant will help me do the homework at school or make a plan of when I can do it.

If I get a detention, it will be a time to be able to get the homework done.

This is okay.

People who can help me

Mrs _____ in room _____.

Mr _____ my form tutor in room _____.

Miss _____ my TA in room _____.

Daily transitions

"I was really scared of the corridors. All the noise and so many people made my brain scream. I couldn't focus on where I was going and so I hid until everyone had gone. I was always late for lessons."

Girl with ASC, Year 7

Once a student with ASC has started at secondary school it is common for them to take longer than most students to be able to settle in to the routines of changing rooms between lessons and coping with the different teachers that they meet throughout the day. Some students will need escorting (by a TA or other students) to each class for some time. Others may benefit from being allowed to leave each class early to avoid the sensory overload of the corridors and travel to their next class in the quieter corridors. In Year 7 a 'buddy system' may be set up so that students with ASC are not left behind when a class moves on.

Teachers should be aware that it can take some time for the student to adjust to their voice, subject matter and style when they have just come from another teacher who may be very different. Subject teachers can support this by:

- having a seating plan and allowing the student with ASC to choose where they sit (where they are comfortable, with a friend, can see the main focus of the lesson, get to the door easily, etc.)
- giving the student time to settle – longer than other students, speaking to them kindly to remind them where they are and which subject they are now doing
- getting to know the student, talking to them about their interests and using this as a basis for a relationship. They will appreciate you for it.

The first few weeks

It is important that a key person is able to check with the student and their teachers how they are settling in, that they have the right skills to organise themselves, and identify any problems early on. There are key issues to check in those first few weeks that may not be issues for students without ASC. This checklist is a guide to review how the student with ASC is settling into secondary school and can be completed by the SENCO or form tutor with the student and their teachers' input. The idea of this is to highlight any areas that could be supported early on before they become major problems. The checklist can be filled in by the student's form tutor or Year leader, and the student themselves may contribute (**see the early weeks checklist on the CD-ROM**). This can identify to the SENCO or form tutor that the student may need extra support in these areas early enough for them to be dealt with.

"I wanted to join in with the other kids and make friends but they all seemed to be friends already and so I just ended up hanging around behind them. I kept losing my planner and forgetting my PE kit. By the time I got home I was so stressed that I couldn't do my homework. After about ten detentions, I finally got help. Now I do my homework at school and am in a lunchtime games group, I'm finally making friends."

Boy with Asperger's, Year 7

CHAPTER 3
Accessing classwork

"My English teacher started to teach us about things like perseverance. I didn't know what it was before, but now I know when I'm struggling I can try to persevere by thinking about it myself, asking someone on my table, or asking my teacher. I think I get a lot more work done now because I'm not afraid to persevere."

Girl with Asperger's, Year 8

Secondary teachers can only be certain that every student with ASC will be different. Students with ASC can be very academically able, possibly exceptionally gifted in certain subjects, but still have many challenges to overcome in accessing the curriculum and completing classwork they should be capable of, to the standard that is expected.

Difficulties with understanding verbal communication, executive functioning (planning, organising, monitoring, focusing), sensory distortion and overload, rigid thinking and obsessive interests can impact on students' ability to engage with classwork. The challenge of coping with different classrooms and different teachers each with their own style of teaching, tone of voice and teaching strategies can also mean that the effort needed to cope with all these changes and adjustments can leave little energy left to focus and concentrate on the actual lesson and complete work tasks. Other students can have learning disabilities and other conditions such as dyslexia, dyspraxia, dyscalculia or other difficulties that impair their learning. By supporting their needs in the classroom we are aiming to develop more independent working, but this may take some time and consistency to achieve.

Difficulties with verbal communication

Much of the teaching done in secondary school is verbal. Teachers talk, explain, instruct, ask questions and discuss with their students. This is done with the assumption that their students have reached a certain level of development in their understanding and ability to communicate. Secondary teachers expect that students will understand basic concepts, be able to think about abstract ideas and take on board a variety of perspectives. They will assume that most students can compose different pieces of writing such as a report, story, account or instructions. Students will be expected to be able to ask and answer questions, draw conclusions and understand sarcasm, jokes and where to 'draw the line'. Of course, teachers understand that in every class there will be students who struggle with some of these abilities but for students with ASC, verbal communication can be difficult to understand, keep up with and contribute to. Students with ASC may speak fluently and use long words, but their speech may be rambling and lacking in clarity of purpose and direction. They may want to speak only about things that are important to themselves and need help to learn about appropriate speech, tone and volume. They may interrupt, call out or argue that others are saying the wrong things, or be too quiet and reluctant to speak in class at all. There are many issues that can affect a student with ASC:

- difficulties 'tuning in' to the teacher when there is background noise, flickering lights, others moving about the room. Smells, such as strong perfume or deodorant, sweaty PE shoes and disinfectant can lead to stress and inability to concentrate.
- difficulties keeping up with the pace of spoken communication; for example, the number of instructions given out before starting a piece of work. Slower processing time means that they can be still trying to understand what the first thing you said was, when you have moved on to the next or further examples.
- difficulty understanding the inferred and assumed meaning of what has been said, especially if using sarcasm or jokes
- difficulty looking at the teacher at the same time as listening. Many students with ASC cannot do both, and you may need to accept this, but then they can miss facial expressions, body language, gestures that the teacher uses to enhance their communication.
- difficulty understanding what the important part of the information is. They may not be able to see the 'big picture', instead becoming easily overwhelmed with all the irrelevant details.
- having literal understanding may mean that they do not comply with general instructions such as *Everyone do this*, as they may not see themselves as being 'everyone'.
- difficulty in being verbally able to ask for help. This often causes students with ASC to sit for long periods of time not doing anything. Being told to *Get on with it* does not help.
- difficulty in understanding the point of what you have been saying. Some students with ASC are literal and rigid in their opinions and find others' opinions difficult to accept. In some subjects such as history, RE and English this can cause arguments and a refusal to engage with the work.
- learning objectives may be meaningless to the student with ASC. They need to see the point of what they are doing and how it links to an end result. Many students with ASC have narrow interests and will struggle to see the point of learning anything in subjects they do not like. Learning for learning may need to be a taught skill.

What subject teachers can do

- Encourage social greetings, manners and respectful and complimentary speech with all students and encourage all to reply to social greetings.
- Try to avoid rushing or suddenly asking questions of the student with ASC. Give them warning that it is their turn next to answer a question.
- Don't expect eye contact or appropriate facial expression if they don't seem to do this naturally. You will often realise that a student with ASC listens better when eye contact is not an issue. If they need to look at the whiteboard or illustration whilst

listening, tell them that's what they need to do and give them more time to process what you are saying or give them their own copy of the illustration on their desk.

- Be clear and direct when giving instructions. Use the words *First, Then, Next, Finally* to structure your instructions but only give the student as many as they can handle at a time. Writing these on the board as a list works well for all students.
- Say their name first if you want their attention but don't make them stand out by using it too often.
- Say what you do want rather than what you don't want (e.g. '*Please walk in the corridor*' rather than '*Don't run*' or '*I want you to sit quietly and listen to me*' rather than '*Stop messing about*').
- Say exactly how a piece of work can be improved rather than leave it open-ended for the student to work out.
- Explain the hidden meaning where possible – what is being inferred or referred to.
- Find out what interests and motivates your students with ASC. Discover their skills and strengths and give them projects in which they can use these interests and gifts.
- Try to show the student the whole picture of the topic you are studying. Show them the term's plans and learning objectives and work with them to set personal learning targets in steps that they can see as relevant to them. Explain the curriculum to them and how they are moving along in the subject. Do this through mapping it out visually where possible.
- Tell them what they are learning and teach them how to learn. Use concepts such as perseverance, resilience, resourcefulness, collaboration, planning, evaluating and communicating ideas and focus on one at a time, teaching what it is, exploring how to do it and reminding the students of where they can use the skill.

Organising and planning a task

"The best lessons were where the teachers wrote a list of what we were supposed to do on the board. It sounds so simple but I could keep checking what I had to do instead of trying to remember it and do the work at the same time."

Boy with ASC, Year 9

The poor executive functioning ability of some students with ASC tends to be most obvious when attempting classwork. They can misunderstand instructions and not know how to ask for help, find it difficult to know how long a task should take or how much they should do. Finding the right equipment, knowing how or where to start and maintaining the plan in mind whilst carrying it out in order to complete a piece of classwork can be overwhelming and stressful for them. It is common for even the brightest children with ASC to find strategies to hide the fact that they cannot plan and organise a task successfully. This is when we may see students use strategies to avoid doing the work, such as refusing, distracting others, fidgeting, being quiet and doing nothing or copying the work of others.

Some students with ASC may excel at planning a task they are interested in. They may go to great lengths and detail and come up with excellent ideas and solutions to problems if they can see the point of what they are doing. Design and technology (DT) subjects can be good for students with these skills but it is better that they are given choices of what to make rather than a specific object that may mean nothing to them. In the same way some students excel at maths or story writing or science because of their ability to plan and problem solve in great detail.

What subject teachers can do

- Spend some time getting to know the student with ASC. Personally overseeing their teaching and progress in class will be advantageous in you gaining an understanding of what works best for them and will provide valuable support to the TA in supporting the student effectively.
- Accept that some students with ASC may need fidget toys, stress balls or another sensory activity to help their central nervous system become more organised. Consider allowing fidget toys (with suitable boundaries) so that a student can be ready to work.
- Where the student sits may need careful planning and can make a lot of difference. Make sure you ask them where they would prefer to sit and consider sensory issues such as lighting, noise and smells as well as good role models in other children to sit with. Don't suddenly change where they are sitting.
- Clear, structured and chunked work helps enormously. This can be as simple as folding the worksheet into sections, drawing a border around different sections of work or providing a structural writing/planning framework for the piece of work.
- Provide clear behaviour expectations that explain to a student what is required and gives them praise or rewards for being focused and completing each part of the work. (For more on supporting behaviour see Chapter 8.)
- Give the student a way to communicate with you that they do not understand, without it looking obvious to other students. Traffic light systems, a communication card, a Social Story™ or a simple taught phrase can support a student to ask for help. These can be useful for students with ASC who do not like or need a TA 'hovering' around them all the time.
- Know the student's stress signs and don't take arrogance or rudeness personally. Students will need reminding of appropriate manners but will respond better when they are less anxious and successful in their work. Use humour that they can understand and take an interest in their special interests to build up a rapport with them. Try to build in positive interactions so that when negative issues have to be approached they might respond better.
- Use visual strategies wherever possible. Photos, pictures, diagrams, charts and mind maps can really help a student with ASC 'see' what they are learning. Lists, role-play and DVD modelling can be really helpful. Using speech and thought bubbles to explore characters' thoughts, feelings and motives can be useful in subjects such as English, RE, history and drama.
- Some students with ASC have excellent memories and can learn well by rote; others may need lists of the important points to remember or include in a piece of work. You may get very logical and literal answers to questions because of their concrete understanding. When you need more than this, give them support by first asking factual questions and then more open questions using '*how*' and '*why*'. They may need some extra support in learning to answer questions that require more detail.
- Teach students how to work with others before you start introducing group work. Start with how to work with a partner and then move on to working in threes and

then a larger group. Accept that for some students with ASC group work may always be very difficult for them and working with a calm and confident partner may be more successful. Allow them to work on their own too, if that means that the piece of work is completed well.

"I can't work in a group. I end up having to be in complete control because I can't cope with anyone else having ideas. It has to be my way or nothing and I can get really angry if the others don't do it. It's the only way I can cope, but of course, it usually ends up in a big row and I get into trouble. I'd rather work on my own."
Boy with Asperger's, Year 8

Difficulties with writing

Writing can be one of the most difficult issues for a student with ASC and writing is required in almost every school subject. Some students with ASC have an extreme aversion to writing, others will only write the minimum they can, but others may really love writing and be able to write long and in-depth pieces of work. However, checking, correcting and redrafting may be something they cannot contemplate because in their mind the work is finished. Some are consumed by perfectionism and refusal comes through fear of failure. Some may have sensory-motor difficulties where the motor skill of writing has always been difficult for them. Some may have co-existing conditions such as dyslexia or dyspraxia.

The first questions should be whether the student is capable of writing and what issues are preventing them from writing and then the correct support can be put in place which may look very different for each student. These may be some of the strategies that can be used to support writing:

For students who don't know what to write about or are not interested in writing

- Where possible, begin with allowing the student to write factual accounts or be able to include subjects that interest them. It works well if a student can learn to be successful by writing about their special interests before introducing other subjects and genres. They may struggle to write from other points of view so it is better to adapt this to make the writing more accessible.
- Teach the student to use mind maps or other ways of making notes about their ideas. Writing frames can be really useful, but students will need to be taught how to plan in bullet points so that they are not writing so much in the plan that there is nothing left to write in the actual task.
- Use cloze sentences for the student to fill in key words rather than copy large chunks of text from the board or textbook. This will help with comprehension.
- Give visual guidelines as to how much writing you expect. Make sure this is achievable: it is better to start with a shorter expectation, be successful and build up to a greater length slowly.
- Limit the amount of copying off the board that your students do. For students with ASC it is better to give them a printout of the text and a highlighter so that they can read the text, underline the key words or phrases and have the time to understand what the text is about. This can be particularly helpful in geography, science, history

and other subjects. It gives the student that extra processing time and is a strategy that can help many students.

- Be creative in using different forms of recording in your lessons. Ask yourself, '*Does this have to be written down?*'. There may be practical ways students can show what they are learning: charts, diagrams, cartoons, pictures, collage of articles that they write speech bubbles about, sequencing cards (e.g. putting the water cycle into correct sequence), making models, using construction sets to model stories or events, role-play, video recording and using ICT. Students may find typing easier or be able to use apps that allow them to dictate or draw onto a tablet computer and record their work that way. This provides variety and takes the pressure off students for whom writing is always very stressful.

- Teach the student with ASC that it is okay to ask for clarification and help when they don't understand something. Rather than having an adult 'hovering' around them you could use a planned signal or piece of card that they put on their desk when they need help.

For students who have difficulty with the motor skills of writing

It is hoped that the student will have received support to work on their writing skills in primary school and there are many good, structured schemes that are very useful. However, a student may not have the sensory feedback in their nervous system to write well or the motor-organisation skills to do so. There are different opinions on the importance of handwriting, but by the time the student is in secondary school the sheer volume of writing expected can cause them to fall behind in their learning. There is evidence that writing things down improves the ability to remember what has been written and so some writing skill needs to be encouraged in students with ASC.

> *"Handwriting is a complex skill involving a wide range of cognitive, linguistic, perceptual and motor abilities... At secondary school, children are obliged to write almost constantly, taking notes to dictation, writing essays, and copying down the homework required for the next day. For the child who has learned to form letters without apparent deliberation or effort, such tasks are straightforward. In contrast, for the child who is still struggling with the basic elements of the skill then even copying down homework may present a problem."*
>
> Henderson & Green, National Handwriting Association (2016)

Often handwriting does not improve at secondary school without extra lessons to practise it. Parents may take this on board and do extra work at home, but all teachers should consider providing alternative ways of recording for some of the many writing tasks they ask students to do. This has the benefit of giving the student many ways of recording and the chance to find a strategy that works well for them. Some examples are:

- using a laptop to be able to type longer pieces of work. Students should have good keyboard skills or be given a keyboard programme to do at home to develop this.
- writing frames, cloze sentences, speech bubbles, cartoon strips, flow charts, grids, charts and pictograms, timelines, mind maps, bullet points, highlighting key words, labelling. All these methods show understanding and learning but use fewer words.

- using speech apps (e.g. Dragon Dictate) on a tablet. These can be very useful but students will need to be able to organise what they want to write and will still need to learn planning techniques such as bullet points or mind maps.
- visually students could take photos, sequence pictures to write about a process (e.g. a science experiment), make a film, use PowerPoint or make a model. Let them choose their favourite construction material.
- a scribe – some students do have a TA to scribe for them but in the longer term this may be detrimental to them. It is best to identify some types of work the student can attempt independently and which ones require a scribe. It can work well if the student is paired with another student who is a good writer for some joint tasks.

Obsessive interests

Many students with ASC have specialist areas of knowledge and interest. These can be as wide ranging as there are things to be interested in, but the common factor is that these special interests bring pleasure and are an area of intense passion and focus. Girls and boys with ASC may share common interests with their peers, such as video games, horses and animals, but may have intense and in-depth focus on these topics. They may want to talk about them all the time, bring every conversation around to their particular interest, and want to talk about or be involved in their interest to the exclusion of all other activity. Some special interests may seem untypical for students in a secondary school and so the reactions from other students when the student with ASC wants to talk about those things are negative or unresponsive. Students with ASC can be teased, bullied, called names and left out because of their interests and obsessive behaviours. It can also lead to obsessions that are focused on particular people such as a girl who 'fancies' a boy and follows him everywhere.

Obsessive interests can be the only thing that brings positive emotions into the life of a student with ASC and it is important not to take this pleasure away from them unless it is unhealthy, destructive or harmful to others. This can take a lot of work, using Social Stories™ to help the student understand the different points of view as to why the particular interest is not appropriate. For example, a student who talks about guns, killing and war may need to learn the difference between reality and fiction (particularly in relation to video games), and a student who is obsessed by another student may need to understand more about appropriate relationships, consent and personal space.

When special interests become obsessive, they can impact on the student's social relationships with their peers. It can cause others to be bored of their company, lead to arguments about who is right or knows more, and can be so engrossing for the student with ASC that they do not engage with other events and situations with other students.

> *"I wanted to sit with the girls at lunchtime because they were nice. I told them all about my favourite film. None of them had watched it so I told them everything that happened from the start to the finish. My TA said, did I not notice that they were bored? I felt embarrassed then. I had no idea they were bored."*
>
> Boy with Asperger's, Year 9

What subject teachers can do

- If a special interest is appropriate, allow the student to bring their specialist knowledge into the subject and their work. For example, let them do their English talks about their interest. If they love trains, let them use timetables to work out maths problems. If other students have a similar interest, try to foster friendship between them and the student with ASC by allowing them to sit together and work as partners.

- Teach conversation and discussion skills in a structured way. Work in pairs to begin with and encourage students to find out something about their partner, such as what do they think about an idea or issue, what their preferences are and what they are interested in, linked to the subject topic. Be aware that conversation is likely to remain a difficulty for students with ASC throughout their adult lives and so do not put too much pressure on them; allow them to listen to others and praise them when they do join in appropriately (without making them stand out amongst their peers).

- Encourage students with ASC to foster friendships with others who may have similar interests and to join school or outside clubs which can develop their social skills through mutual hobbies.

- Show how their interests can link to other areas and to the curriculum where possible. One teacher helped a boy whose interest was farming and livestock breeding to learn all the farming terms in French and then developed this into French conversation skills so that he could imagine talking to a French farmer.

- Remember that their special interests are strengths and can lead to careers. One student with ASC was obsessed with pipes and wires. He became the helper to the school caretaker and eventually became an apprentice electrician. All through his secondary education his interest was praised and encouraged by the school, whilst a programme of social skills teaching was also in place to help him learn how to communicate well with his workmates and customers.

CHAPTER 4
Advice for subject teachers

English

English is a core subject that develops language and communication skills – the very skills that students with ASC may have difficulty with because of their condition. The curriculum requires students to understand and interpret many aspects of language and how it is communicated, from different genres of texts as well as to compose their own writing accurately, creatively and with different audiences in mind.

As with all subjects some students with ASC will do well in English, finding that the structured and supported learning of language and prose suits them well. There are many students with ASC who have very creative story-telling skills, love to read and, with support, can be helped to speak publically. They may, however, find the more subtle nuances and inference of language difficult to grasp due to literal interpretation. Jokes, sarcasm, idioms and similes may be difficult to understand and they may need support to understand language in this kind of depth.

However, many students with ASC struggle greatly in English lessons because of their difficulties with communication, flexible thinking and imagining what something might be like. They can find it difficult to imagine someone else's point of view and take on multiple perspectives. Writing can seem a torturous activity to them, from the motor skill of writing to the organisation and structure of ideas and planning and the understanding of plot, perspective and inference. In English lessons there are more specific considerations and support that can be given to students with ASC:

Reading

Every student with ASC will be different in their ability to read. Some will devour books and hide away in their stories and worlds they are reading about, and then have strong opinions on what they have read. Other good readers may find it difficult to express what they have been reading about, especially the incentives and emotions of the character and inferred meanings within the story. Others may only read factual books and be a mine of information about their chosen topics, way beyond their peers (and sometimes their teachers!). There are many more students with ASC who find reading very difficult and will often just refuse to do it. They may have had years of failure, had undiagnosed dyslexia, or just find that what they are being asked to read makes no sense to them.

Teachers need to check reading comprehension skills in students with ASC. These children can easily misunderstand a text or take what they read literally. They may read fluently without understanding the text or being able to recall what they read. Reading comprehension skills will need supporting with inference and narrative skills as well as help with social understanding.

A student with ASC may find that fiction does not make sense to them because they do not understand the social implications in the story. They may need targeted support to help them learn about inference and 'making guesses' based on the clues in the text. Regular comprehension exercises on short pieces of text can help improve their understanding.

Even choosing a book from the school library can be overwhelming for a student with ASC because there is too much choice. If a child refuses to read it is a good idea to give them a box of books to choose from which includes books they have read before, factual books on their particular interests, comics and graphic books, and a few new books that may have a connection to something they are interested in.

Every lesson requires some reading, and in English there are many texts and genres to have to deal with. There are writing, speaking and listening demands that go with the reading and as ASC is a social communication disability, then English is often one of the most demanding lessons for the student. Often students with ASC have limited general knowledge and life experiences to draw upon to assist them in their understanding. Poor executive function skills mean that organising, sequencing and holding key information in their memory can be very difficult for them.

Strategies for the teacher

- Give students more time to read things, and give them a highlighter pen to help them remember key points, ideas and the sequence of the story or report. Provide an overview of the different types of text and what their purposes are. Support students in finding key points that meet this purpose.
- Use ICT. Computers, apps and the internet are motivating and have an enormous amount of English curriculum-related content. Plan this in and consider apps such as those from Claro Software (others are available) which read out the text to the student. Recording themselves and listening to it back can help with retention. This can be good for homework using a tablet computer or phone app.
- Use visuals to support the story. Timelines, sequence of pictures, character maps, word banks that explain phrases, metaphors and idioms can all help. If there is a film of the book and it is fairly accurate, lend students the DVD to watch at home before they read the book.
- When searching for meaning or character traits, use the 'social detective' strategy (see Chapter 6) and look for the clues. This will support the student's social understanding.

Writing

To compose a piece of writing requires a student to plan, organise, remember things, prioritise, self-monitor, pay attention and use information and experiences from the past to solve current problems – a difficult set of skills for a student with ASC who struggles with poor executive functioning skills.

Students with ASC may find it difficult to draw on previous experiences and lack the flexibility of thought to apply previous knowledge to a new task. The difference between fact and opinion can be difficult, as is having to comment on their own work, and others' demands that they are able to understand what the teacher is looking for and what the writer actually means. Taking notes is a skill which requires a student to be able to listen, process what is being said and write it down quickly whilst listening to the next piece of information. This is often very stressful for many students with ASC. Copying from the board involves switching attention from the paper to the board and always being able to find where you are up to – again, a great difficulty for many on the autistic spectrum.

Strategies for the teacher

- Break up the writing task into manageable chunks. Draw a box on a blank piece of paper to show how much students should write. Story frames also help break a task into chunks.
- Structure the writing by giving the student a set of questions to answer. Give guidance to how long the answers should be. Teach them about open and closed questions and what is expected. Show good examples. At first you may get some copying of ideas until they gain confidence to try their own idea but it will help writing get going.
- Give students writing tasks related to their particular interests wherever possible until they build up their confidence in the genre or style, then you can introduce writing about different topics. Allow students with ASC to use ideas from their favourite films and stories when writing their own. Encourage them to change key factors such as setting, character names and consequences.
- Let the student use a computer to enable them to redraft and edit work. It is a lot easier on a computer and they can save previous drafts for assessment. If using a computer to do written tasks make it mandatory that printing out has to be completed. Where possible, make sure there is easy access to a printer and print it out in lesson time. Leaving it for break time, lunchtime or home time only puts more organisational pressure on the student.

Speaking and listening

We have already outlined the nature of the communication difficulties that many students with ASC have, and whether they have poor language skills or can talk at great length, having to do structured speaking and listening tasks in a lesson may be difficult for all. The social interaction skills needed to speak to an audience, wait for your turn to speak and adapt your language for the listeners can also be overwhelming. Accepting and understanding other people's points of view, possibly having a narrow range of interests, poor listening skills, an inability to read and use non-verbal communication and anxiety about all those things, can mean that speaking in front of others seems impossible. Some students with ASC cannot judge the intonation and pace needed, use gestures and non-verbal communication effectively and know when they need to pause to let others speak. Discussion, debate and group work can be very difficult for many students with ASC. However, with support they can learn many skills, including conversation and public speaking.

Strategies for the teacher

- Do as much preparation for the student's verbal exercises as possible. Agree the topic, structure the talk with them and practise. Show them how to use tone of voice, posture, gestures, space and pace.
- Use role-play and drama to teach and practise speaking and listening skills with the whole class. Puppets and masks can be a good way to help the student with ASC think about the skills they need to communicate with others.

- Let the student use a tablet computer or other device to video themselves and watch it back. Remember to first say what they are doing well and encourage more of that whilst making one suggestion at a time of what they could add to it.
- Watch TED Talks (free online talks advertised as 'ideas worth spreading') or other public speakers and debates to help the students observe effective skills.
- Visual support such as crib cards and a visual sequence of pictures on a PowerPoint that the student has made can illustrate their speech and take the pressure off remembering what comes next.
- Choose topics that the student with ASC knows something about whenever possible. Give them video links to watch before a discussion or debate to familiarise them with the topic. This can be of two opposing opinions if necessary.
- Don't assume that the student with ASC understands what you mean, especially if you use sarcasm, metaphors or shared experiences you are assuming your class will have had. Use these forms of communication but explain what you are doing. For example, say '*I was being sarcastic when I said…*'. Always keep in mind how what you say can be taken literally and be mindful of explaining yourself or the metaphor more clearly.

Mathematics

Number

Some students with ASC are very good at maths. Often they like the structured and logical nature of the subject and quickly see patterns and connections in numbers, shapes and measures. Others struggle to grasp maths concepts or apply their numerical knowledge to number word problems. Their communication difficulties may impair their ability to follow instructions and understand complex explanations. Some students with ASC are so good at number operations that they can be way ahead of their peers, and some are even so good that difficulties arise when they are asked to show their working out. If they just 'know' the answer, then writing down a computation means nothing to them and this can often lead to stress or arguments with teachers. Algebra can be difficult to grasp as the abstract nature of a symbol standing for a number can seem meaningless to the student. Estimation, approximation and applying one concept to another situation relies heavily on the student's flexible thought and memory skills – a fundamental difficulty for students with ASC.

Shape, space and measure

Students with ASC may have visual perception difficulties which can cause them to find shape and space difficult to recognise and work with. Others may be excellent in this topic and have a real strength in understanding the features, properties and concepts of shape and space. For those who have difficulty the key is to break down and structure activities, check understanding and support students with practical and visual activities.

Recognising detail and shapes in the environment may be a strength in some students with ASC, but others may not be able to generalise so easily. Some students with ASC will not have the flexibility of thought to do this and so it will take more structured and repetitive teaching to embed the concepts of shape, space and measure that they need to learn. Once the complexity of using and applying shape, space and measure increases, the student with ASC may then have difficulty plotting graphs and shapes and working with angles and areas. Following formulas may be a strength, but understanding how they work may need more support.

Using and applying maths

When we think about using maths to solve everyday problems, students with ASC may find it difficult because they are presented with a word problem on a worksheet and may not make the connection between the word problem and the real-life situations that require maths knowledge or skills. Basically, students with ASC need to see the point of what you are asking them to do.

Strategies for the teacher

- When introducing maths word problems begin with ones that are simple and logical and do not have lots of unrelated information in them. If it helps, make them about the student's special interests to motivate them.
- Homework activities can focus on the practical use of maths. Students can do practical tasks that involve numbers with their parents (such as adding up, shopping, counting how many items they have, and working out how much is needed).
- Whenever possible show the class/student a practical example of the maths concept you are using. These can be found online or done practically in class. Use, model and repeat mathematical vocabulary regularly. Ask students to tell you what vocabulary fits with the task they are doing.
- Use apps or computer programmes for shape and space and to develop perspective of 3D shapes. Other maths programmes can be used to develop understanding and many use games to gain interest. Check that the student with ASC has understood the concept rather than just following a process blindly.
- Allow extra processing time for mental maths and don't put students with ASC on the spot to come up with an answer in front of everyone else in the class. If they want to answer all the time and get upset if you don't pick them or shout out a lot, then support them with turn-taking skills. Give them a mini whiteboard so they can prove they did know the answer. This can take away the stress of not being chosen.

Other areas of the curriculum

Every student with ASC will enjoy some subject areas and dislike others. They may have an uneven academic profile and be more inspired by subjects that are practical, artistic, scientific or related to their special interests. The changes to the National Curriculum in 2015 mean students are required to learn a demanding amount in all subjects at a faster pace than previously. Pressure to have evidence and to be able to record their knowledge is enormous, and any difficulty with communication, social interaction, flexible thinking and sensory processing is going to have an impact on a student with ASC's ability to access the curriculum. The testing and assessment regime will be another challenge that may cause anxiety, distress and difficulties for students with ASC. On top of that they have a different teacher for each subject and the dynamics of their relationship with that teacher will have an enormous effect on their performance and engagement in the lesson.

There are often far more barriers to learning for a student with ASC than a neurotypical student. Overcoming the difficulties they may have in English and maths will underpin their success in many other subjects. Indeed, they may excel in subjects that they understand, like and feel successful in. Imaginative teachers can often find a 'way in' for even their most reluctant students once they understand their needs. Outdoor learning, ICT and practical activities can be used in many imaginative ways to support the curriculum.

Below is a summary of the strengths and difficulties students with ASC commonly have in their school subjects.

Science

Strengths	Difficulties
Students with ASC often have a strong interest in, and aptitude for, science. Science is about logical and systematic processes, practical experiments and factual knowledge. Students who love science can be supported to look at other subjects in a scientific way. You may have a student who has superior scientific knowledge (more than the curriculum demands). Some students with ASC may be extremely gifted and talented in science and should be supported to extend and widen their knowledge, skills and understanding of the subject.	Students with poor executive functioning can struggle to follow instructions and carry out an experiment that requires them to draw conclusions from their investigations. They can easily lose where they are up to and will need visual and structured support to be able to carry out an activity. If they are very poor at drawing conclusions they may need to choose from two or three alternatives where only one is likely. Teaching the concepts of *likely* and *unlikely* can also be useful. There may also be some issues with sensory processing in science, so do be aware of situations regarding food, smells, texture, touch, movement and visual focus. Be aware of students with ASC having literal understanding as this impacts on their ability to make inferences and draw conclusions.

Strategies for the teacher

- If a student with ASC is refusing to take part, check that you have prepared them for what is happening, communicated this appropriately (and visually) to them and considered their sensory profile when planning science activities, as sensitivities such as noise, smells and touch can be a barrier to them accessing practical science.
- Write down instructions in steps (such as *First, Then, Finally*). The student may need a copy of the instructions on their desk if they find it difficult to keep looking up at the board and then find the point they are up to.
- Make sure health and safety rules are clearly understood by the student with ASC. Show and practice handling equipment so you are sure they understand. They may take things literally and miss any implied meaning which can sometimes lead to them doing unsafe things without knowing they have done so. Having visual reminders (such as a laminated sheet of safe handling photos in the box of equipment) can be very effective.
- Mind maps and flow diagrams can support understanding of links and outcomes of scientific processes, helping the student see links to previous learning.
- Teach students the investigation questions they should be asking and write these down (e.g. in the front of their book) so that they can refer to them frequently and learn that these questions can be applied to different scientific investigations.

Physical Education (PE)

Strengths	Difficulties
Some students with ASC enjoy the physical nature of PE and seek to run off their pent-up energy with enthusiasm. They are well co-ordinated and well accepted by others who see their talents and want them on their team. For those with good physical skills this can be a relief from the stresses and demands of the classroom, particularly written work. Some individual sports can be a strength and students with ASC can do well in swimming, running and gymnastics where they are not involved in a team. Using gym equipment, circuit training and outdoor sports can encourage students with ASC who find team sport difficult to engage in physical activity.	There are sensory challenges (e.g. getting changed into their PE kit, a large echoing hall, textures, temperatures). Team games involve social demands such as taking turns, co-operation and winning and losing. Competition may not be a concept that they can emotionally cope with. They also need co-ordination skills and the ability to judge distances and make instant decisions. Their sensory difficulties may cause them to be clumsy, unco-ordinated, have fear of others touching them, refuse to get changed or hate wearing pumps or trainers and have great anxiety about doing PE. A change or a new routine can be stressful to students with ASC so a substitute teacher or introducing a new game or skill may cause them difficulty. They need to know what the point of the activity is or be able to 'see' how it happens. A student with ASC may have poor body awareness which can prevent them understanding and communicating how their body feels during different activities. They can be prone to over-heating or being cold without being aware of it.

Strategies for the teacher

- Use video clips to show how to play a new sport or develop a new sport skill.
- For team games explain the point of the game carefully and use video clips to support this. Allow partner work rather than whole team at first. Encourage all students to look for what others do well and encourage one another in sportsmanship.
- Use cones, spot markers and other visual clues to help students understand boundaries, routes and directions.
- Allow some flexibility for sensory issues, such as being able to wear jogging trousers if students are extremely sensitive to temperature or touch, or to get changed in a quiet place if the changing rooms are a source of stress for them.
- Teach them to recognise changes in their bodies and how exercise can reduce stress, as well as the adrenalin rush that comes when they are highly emotional (such as during anger). Give them moves to do at home and websites to explore. Apps that track daily physical exercise can be useful.

History and Geography

Strengths	Difficulties
These may be subjects that are closely related to a student with ASC's special interests. The factual aspect of these subjects may also appeal to them; some students with ASC can memorise huge amounts of factual, historical or geographical data (such as a list of all the British Prime Ministers, or types of rocks and gems). However, in history and geography students with ASC may need many opportunities to put the factual information they know into meaningful context and be able to 'see' how particular events, people or systems fit together. They may have extensive knowledge, be fascinated by strategy and systems and excel at these subjects because they have a strong desire to know everything there is to know about it. Having exceptional knowledge and ability in these subjects can increase a student with ASC's self-esteem and encourage them to develop their literacy skills in a context they feel more confident in.	Some students with ASC may find the concept of time and chronology very difficult to grasp, both in terms of ordering events in the past and in imagining what an unfamiliar place or environment might be like. They may also need support in the organisation and imagination required to write about unfamiliar concepts and events. Students who find English tasks difficult may resist more writing during other lessons and although they may be able to read competently, may find it difficult to extract the key points and implied meaning in history and geography texts. They can find it difficult to see the whole picture and make links between other key points covered in past learning. Conversely, those who struggle to read may have little motivation for the subjects that demand them to do even more reading and which have unfamiliar vocabulary. Students with ASC may need support to reflect on the meaning of events and consider their impact and different points of view surrounding them in history – they may find it difficult to imagine themselves in an historical context as 'they don't live there'. One of the most difficult challenges for teachers in these subjects is to engage students who are not interested in them and so don't see the point.

Strategies for the teacher

➢ Help students with ASC to engage with history and geography through visuals, practical experiences, role-play, outside visits, pictures and ICT. These should have reference points and start with things that are familiar to them. Students can then add the new information in in relation to that.

➢ Start with a topic or area that the student is familiar with and try to help them see connections and links with subsequent topics. Explaining the point of what they are learning and finding connections with their interests and knowledge will support motivation in the subjects.

➢ Be aware that language may be taken literally and not to assume that a student with ASC will get any inferred meaning as you explain things to the class. Pictures and video clips can help illustrate points more clearly to them. They will likely need extra support to accept and work with abstract concepts and differing points of view.

➢ Teach the key concepts step by step, explain the difference between fact and opinion and which sources or data can be trusted or need to be checked out. This may need more support than for other students, with real examples being used to illustrate the points.

Design and Technology (DT)

Strengths	Difficulties
Students with ASC are often extremely proficient at using technology and can become very competent with computers, tablets or laptops. They may also have practical skills in construction and design ideas and be artistic, which can mean that design and technology subjects are successful areas of the curriculum for them. They may enjoy creative subjects that are more practical, such as food technology and resistant materials, and be much more engaged than when in lessons that demand a lot more writing. Some students with ASC are excellent at seeing logical systems and detailed connections and so electronics can be a strength. They may have spent years being able to build complex models and use mechanical engineering at home and so feel confident in using construction materials at school.	Students with ASC may need support to follow stepped instructions and can easily rush ahead as they get involved in practical or computer-based tasks or activities without reflecting on what they are being asked to do. Sensory or motor difficulties can be a barrier to doing practical DT tasks and teachers should be aware of the student with ASC's needs and abilities. Some students find the design process too hard and will therefore refuse to begin or will incorporate the ideas of others. It can be useful to support them with a choice of pictures and visual ideas to begin with, rather than asking them to create something from scratch. Difficulty with prediction or forming a hypothesis may mean that they cannot plan a task accurately and carry it out to completion. Evaluation demands many perspective skills they may not have. They may become angry and frustrated easily when a task does not go to plan and can become extremely stressed with deadlines and time constraints.

Strategies for the teacher

▸ Health and safety rules will work best when they are visual. Picture cards with tools and equipment with clear pictures or photos to remind students of safe handling rules are most effective. You can show students that the Toyota car factory is based on visual communication (www.graphicproducts.com/articles/toyota-production-system) and perhaps they could develop their own system as a class at the beginning of the year.

▸ Show students with ASC where to start and how to follow a sequence of instructions, such as a recipe. The more visual the instructions are the more likely the student will be able to follow them.

▸ A student with ASC may find having to evaluate their product very difficult. Start by giving them a list of simple questions that give a yes/no answer before asking them to suggest how the 'no' answers can be developed.

▸ Students with ASC may not be able to foresee the consequences of their actions or activities when working in designing and making products. They may need help to predict outcomes and seeing a finished product will help them see what they should be aiming for.

▶ Sensory and special awareness difficulties can lead to potential accidents and misuse of equipment. Some equipment may distress a student who has a high sensitivity to noise, smells, touch or visual stimuli, for example. Be aware of this and make adaptations (such as letting them wear ear defenders or gloves, or being able to leave the room when it is too much).

Information and Communication Technology (ICT)/Computer Science

Strengths	Difficulties
Students with ASC can be gifted in using computers and feel most confident in this subject. They may have superior skills to their peers and know a lot about technical aspects of computing as well as the programming and software that is used in lessons. Students with ASC may have skills in particular areas such as gaming and video production which can be harnessed to develop creative projects such as animation or film production for the school. They may be very involved in online gaming communities such as Minecraft or Steam-based games and may learn co-operation, design and communication skills through these interests. Some students are very good at seeing where in a system there is a glitch and be very good at programming and even 'hacking', which may need to be acknowledged and discussed with them.	When using computers, students with ASC can easily become fixated on what they want to do or a game they want to play and ignore what they have been asked to do. They can also find it difficult to share a computer or work on a joint task with another student as the social communication demands, paired with the task demands, may be overwhelming. They may easily become bored if the task does not seem to have a point and complain or secretly try to do something they would prefer to be doing. In programming and computer science, robotics and non-game related lessons, the student with ASC may find their executive functioning difficulties cause them problems with planning, organising, sequencing and predicting the outcomes, and so they may become very frustrated with the open-ended nature of the tasks. Students with ASC may find problem solving and working out where they may have gone wrong very difficult. The pace of learning can be overwhelming for some as they seek to understand the steps and implications of a task.

Strategies for the teacher

▶ Teach internet rules and safety in a format students with ASC can understand. Childnet have produced ASC-friendly safety rules called The STAR Toolkit. Refer to these regularly and don't assume the student with ASC will be able to apply these rules whilst on the computer unaided.

▶ Working on a computer can enable a student with ASC to produce work that is set out well, spelt correctly and visual which develops their strengths. Encourage them to edit and use editing functions in different programmes to develop flexibility and creative ways of presenting their work.

▶ Use real-life situations for problem-solving tasks and, where possible, make it relevant to students' interests and experiences.

▶ Use video, YouTube clips and self-help blogs to help a student with ASC understand a concept or task and its applications.

▶ Explore skills such as making videos, animations and presentations to encourage partner work and sharing of ideas with others. Set up a class blog or YouTube channel to share work and get feedback (moderated by the teacher). A class Facebook page or Twitter feed can be a good way to teach appropriate social media skills and help students link up with other schools doing similar projects. A student with ASC could develop social skills by interacting with others online under supervision, and could communicate using their PowerPoint or animation skills.

▶ Set up lunchtime or after-school computer clubs and encourage social skills through different activities. Allow space for students with ASC to 'do their own thing' within the boundaries of safety that you establish. Sharing what they have done can increase communication confidence.

Music

Strengths	Difficulties
Students with ASC can respond positively to music and some have good rhythm, fluency and aptitude in the subject. Students with ASC can follow the structured elements of musical patterns and can have good musicality. They may have a good singing voice and a memory for lyrics and notation. Some will have an 'ear' for playing musical instruments and following musical notation well. Practising and performing music along with their peers can develop social confidence and learning an instrument can develop skills outside having to write and remember facts and concepts. Joining a school choir or band can help with students' social inclusion and build their confidence too.	Sound sensitivity will affect some students with ASC, especially when the class is composing their own music with a variety of instruments. (This can seem overwhelmingly noisy and chaotic to students with ASC.) They may be able to wear noise-reducing headphones, or you may need to make sure that you spread students out to different areas so that each group can hear themselves more clearly. Interpreting music may be difficult for students with ASC as they often have difficulty imagining what something will be like, which may affect communicating their ideas and guessing the meaning of a piece of music. Composing their own music may be hard if they find it difficult to imagine, plan and structure their ideas.

Strategies for the teacher

▶ If a student with ASC is struggling to interpret and compose music they can be given picture choices and listen to ideas from others before making their own choices. Use ICT software to help with structuring a composition.

▶ Be aware of noise sensitivities and allow them to wear headphones or leave the room if overstimulated. Warning of noises to come can help in some cases as can silent pauses or listening to music on individual headphones to reduce arousal.

▶ When performing, allow students with ASC to listen to others first and perform to a smaller group if they are not confident performing in front of the whole class.

Art and Design

Strengths	Difficulties
Some students with ASC can be brilliant artists and welcome the break from writing in other subjects. Art – and drawing in particular – can be a favourite activity of some students. Some have a strong (even photographic) visual memory, which can translate into detailed and accurate artistic representations. Students who cannot speak very well can immerse themselves in an artistic activity and produce work that does not have rigid outcomes and expectations. For some students with ASC drawing can be a means of communication, taking the pressure off them to verbally articulate what they want to say.	When a student with ASC finds unstructured and open-ended activities overwhelming, art can be a subject with too little direction and they can be afraid of 'getting it wrong'. Being unable to generate ideas can prevent them from engaging in the activity. Other issues are sensory; texture and messiness can be too much for students to cope with and they can become very distressed. Planning, creating ideas and evaluating theirs or others' work can be very difficult and cause great stress when the answers may be open-ended. Some students with ASC will work very slowly as they process instructions and sequences of putting a piece of work together which means it takes them far longer than the time they have to do it.

Strategies for the teacher

- If a student with ASC is not engaging with art activities, begin with something they can do and will be successful at. Structure the steps of the activity and introduce sensory textures and activities slowly.

- Students may accept new experiences over time or flatly refuse because they cannot cope with the sensory experience. In this case the activity should be adapted so that they can do something more tolerable for them. Watching someone else do the activity (via a video clip or in person) so that they can replicate the activity can also help.

- Copying other pictures or drawings to develop an 'imagination bank' can help some students to gain confidence and 'have a go' in art lessons. Drawing or painting things they know about and are interested in will also help.

- Students with ASC may prefer to work alone rather than in a group and so paired or group working should be introduced with a lot of support, or it may be necessary that students with ASC are allowed to do their own piece of work.

Religious Education (RE)

Strengths	Difficulties
Students with ASC can be very attuned to aspects of faith and religion and find interest and comfort in the structure and routine of religious practices. If they are from a faith-practising family they may be very familiar with some aspects that they are learning about and be able to speak about their own experiences. They may be very interested in structures and rules and be open to accepting the differences practised in different religions.	Understanding abstract concepts may be difficult for students with ASC, and understanding other people's views and opinions when there is no right or wrong answer can cause confusion. The symbolism in religion can be very confusing for a student with ASC who takes things literally. Some students with ASC are literal and rigid in their opinions and find it difficult to accept the opinions of others. In subjects like RE this can cause arguments and a refusal to engage with the work. Seeing the point of what they are doing is important to children with ASC, and in RE it can be difficult to explain at times. If a student does not have a personal belief they may refuse to engage with the subject.

Strategies for the teacher

- Social Stories™ can help students with ASC understand why people follow a religion and have faith, and explain some of the reasons why people do the things they do. Finding social stories that explain these things can be difficult and so you may have to ask a specialist teacher to assist you to do so.
- Try to link new concepts and information to real-life stories and point out familiar activities that the student will be familiar with. Food, clothing and rituals are common to most human beings and the connections can aid understanding or acceptance of religious practices.
- Be factual and use video clips and visual pictures to help the student understand the topic. Give key vocabulary at the beginning of the topic and encourage them to find pictures that show what the vocabulary is or means.
- Prepare for visits to a religious place of worship thoroughly and carefully and write down the behaviour and etiquette that will be expected and why. If there are sensory issues (such as with taking off shoes) speak to the place of worship to see if adaptations can be made. Smell things such as incense before you go and have sensory items to calm the student with you if needed.

Modern Foreign Languages (MFL)

Strengths	Difficulties
Many students with ASC can find the practical learning of a modern foreign language relatively easy. If they are good at rote learning then the vocabulary and phrasing that they learn at primary level is practical and functional, and therefore makes sense to a logical ASC mind. Often teachers will use ICT or pictures to teach MFL, which plays to the learning strengths of students with ASC.	Students who have difficulty with their first language (with receptive and expressive communication) will find using language in social situations and knowing what to say and how to talk to others difficult in a second language. Literal interpretation, conversation and listening skills may be poor, and processing language may take longer than for other students, by which time the teacher has moved on to another sentence. Translating written language relies on interpreting meaning and context and this can cause confusion and stress for the student with ASC.

Strategies for the teacher

- It may be that students with ASC need visuals or scripts to read to help them practise their MFL vocabulary. Putting language in a role-play context (e.g. a French café) might help them see the purpose of the language, but they may need to practise their 'script' with an adult first.
- The more visual support you can give the better. Chunking worksheets and providing pictures to aid understanding and interpretation of the language can help. Writing scripts on cue cards that students can learn and recording themselves speaking can support conversation skills in MFL.
- Working with a partner is often easier than in a group.

Personal, Social and Health Education (PSHE)

This area of the curriculum is non-statutory but represents all the core areas of weakness for students with ASC. Schools should make provision for PSHE – which includes Sex and Relationships Education (SRE) – and will need to take into account the needs of students with ASC when doing so. Social communication, awareness of others, awareness of their community, personal development, belonging and friendships will be important topics for students with ASC, and PSHE targets should be part of their Individual Education Programmes (IEP). (See Chapter 12 for ideas to support students in SRE).

There are other learning skills that students with ASC need to learn in order to access the curriculum, such as communication skills (for conversation and negotiation), organisation and self-help skills, social and co-operative skills, and the ability to cope with sensory and emotional situations. These are all covered in other chapters in this book (Chapter 6 – Social communication and interaction; Chapter 9 – Managing emotions; Chapter 11 – Bullying).

Strengths	Difficulties
Some students with ASC can be extremely insightful when they are asked about the world, communities and morals. They have strong opinions about how the world works, fairness and competition and can speak on issues covered in PSHE with confidence. They may have a strong desire to right wrongs and be part of a bigger community to make things better for others. They can have a strong sense of empathy for those who suffer and who struggle in life. Many students with ASC can be excellent community champions, mentors to younger ASC students and charity workers, given the right opportunities and support.	The abstract nature of PSHE concepts of community, belonging, opinions, emotions and interacting with others can be profoundly challenging for the student with ASC. Their experiences of isolation, difficulty making friendships and being seen as 'different' can make community an extremely abstract concept for them to grasp. They may struggle to communicate their emotions or an understanding of different points of view. Their opinions may be unconventional and rigid at times and they may find it difficult to see opposing viewpoints as equally valid. Students with ASC may also struggle to show empathy. It is a myth that students with ASC don't have empathy; it just may be very difficult for them to perceive what affects others and the intentions people have towards others. Bullying may be a 'live' issue for them and so discussing it in class may be very stressful. They may have a poor sense of danger and ability to risk assess when looking at issues such as internet safety and danger awareness in life situations.

Strategies for the teacher

- Be aware of literal understanding, rigid opinions and misunderstanding of abstract concepts. It may be that students with ASC need bespoke PSHE lessons and interventions in a smaller group where they can be taught topics and skills that they require that other students may not. Emotional understanding, mental wellbeing and discussing risks, problem-solving and safety skills may be needed.
- Be aware of fears and long-held misconceptions that the student with ASC may have. Support them by listening carefully to what they say and asking them to explain why

they think that. They may need support through *Comic Strip Conversations* (Gray, 1994), social stories and other specific interventions to help them understand how they might have misinterpreted something.

▶ Social skills groups support skills and understanding of concepts in PSHE as well as life skills for the student (see Chapter 6).

▶ Concrete examples, real-life stories, video clips and role-play can help in some topics. Researching issues and facts on the computer can be useful if the student is able to sort the information into fact, opinion and not true, as part of a class-based activity.

▶ Look for opportunities for the student with ASC to get involved in the wider school community through harnessing their special interests. Charity work and supporting events with particular 'jobs' can help them feel that they belong. Encourage parents to look for groups outside the school where they can meet others of similar interests and have a role to play in supporting the group.

CHAPTER 5
Homework

Students with ASC can find homework one of the most difficult aspects of being at secondary school. The challenges of settling into a new and large environment, working with different teachers and making new friendships can be such that adding homework to the mix can cause them and their parents much distress. Some children with ASC are rigid to the point that school is school and home is home and the two do not overlap. This can cause nightly battles for parents as they seek to help and support their child to do the homework that has been set, knowing that it is a requirement of their education at secondary school. This can lead to a lot of stress, confusion and anger for the student, especially if detentions for not doing homework are given in consequence. Refusing to do any homework at all is common. Small and simple tasks can easily overwhelm students with ASC because they are unable to understand what is expected of them and the mental block of '*I can't do it*' is often the first barrier to overcome.

Why is homework so difficult for students with ASC?

Poor communication skills

Keeping up with the pace of the verbal homework instructions means that many students with ASC do not write down the homework correctly, do not understand what it is they have to do, and therefore cannot complete the homework given. They can also have very literal understanding of language and often will misunderstand the questions. For example, one student, when given the question '*Can you explain the effect rainfall has on the landscape?*' simply wrote '*Yes*', and wondered why he then received a detention for not answering the question.

Poor organisational skills

Executive function is the ability to organise our thoughts and actions in order to complete a task. It involves being able to plan, sequence, prioritise, direct our attention, manage our time and review our actions so that we can make adjustments if things are not going to plan. Students with ASC may have very poor executive functioning and therefore will find it very difficult to organise themselves independently to do their homework. You will notice this in the classroom and it is reasonable to assume that it will be equally, if not more, difficult for the student at home. Students who are used to adult support at school may not have the skills to organise themselves independently. Some students have complicated or disorganised home environments which can cause difficulty when trying to do homework.

Poor memory

Some students with ASC have photographic memories and can remember every detail and nuance of what was said. However, they cannot pick out the key important facts or summarise the information which often leads to them being unable to apply what they have remembered to a homework task. You may get repetition or rewording of what you taught with no real understanding or application. Other students with ASC may have great difficulty remembering and recalling what they have learned and without support do not seem to be able to produce much work in class, never mind at home.

> *"I think most people have a memory like a library. They learn something and put it away on a shelf which has something like the library Dewey system. When they want to find it again they just need to go to the right shelf, rummage around and there it is. My memory is like someone came and threw all the books into a big heap on the floor."*
>
> Girl with ASC, Year 10 and A* potential student

Stress and anxiety

As discussed in other chapters, stress and anxiety – due to sensory, communication or social issues – may be a massive part of the student with ASC's day at school. Homework can be seen as continuing that stress and anxiety and may leave the student little or no time to be calm and relaxed in the evening. Sleep problems can be caused by the anxiety of coping with school and homework and so a difficult cycle of more stress and anxiety caused by poor sleep and lack of time to regulate their stress levels can occur. It is common for students with ASC to want to escape into their own world of special interests, computer or video games where there are no schoolwork demands as soon as they get home from school, and parents can have a very difficult time in getting them to do their homework at all.

To be able to do homework a student needs to be able to:

1. Listen to instructions and write them down accurately.
2. Locate their homework diary and find the correct date page.
3. Be able to write quickly enough in the time given.
4. Process the instruction and understand what is required.
5. Predict an outcome and make a plan to achieve it.
6. Organise their own time – when to start and how long it should take.
7. Manage multi-part tasks in order and understand and make links where necessary.
8. Read and review what has been done to see if it matches what was asked.
9. Overcome the desire to do something else instead.
10. Remember to put it in their bag on the correct day to hand it in.

Strategies to support the student

In Year 7 especially it is unreasonable to expect a student with ASC to be able to do all their homework independently. If possible, put support in place before they start. A Social Story™ about homework and a meeting with parents to explain the supported approach would be ideal.

It is important to realise that the student with ASC may be handling a lot of stress over the issue of homework. They can be helped by talking about why teachers give homework before a long-term and a short-term target can be set. This helps the student understand that doing homework independently is an expected goal, but you have also shown them the smaller steps and skills they can learn to achieve this goal. Timescales should be added and how success will be evaluated and rewarded.

SMART targets with tangible rewards or achievements work best for students with ASC.

S small
M measurable
A achievable
R realistic
T timed

Target	By when	How we will support this	How we will know it is achieved	Reward for achieving targets
Long term To be able to complete homework in maths, science, history, geography and DT independently To be able to complete homework in English, RE and French with support	The end of Year 7	Smaller steps Record sheet Meeting with parents to see how they can help Homework club two times per week Teachers will make sure I have copied down the homework properly.	Record sheet I will be able to do the homework set and it will be in my books.	
Step 1 To be able to follow a 2–3 step homework task with support, at school and at home	The end of term 1	TA will write the homework in my diary. I will go to homework club two times a week. Teachers will try to give me structured rather than open-ended tasks.	Write homework in three steps Record sheet of what I have done Homework will be in my books	
Step 2 To be able to do a 2–3 step homework task on my own, but support available if I ask for it	The end of term 2	I will write the homework in my diary. I will do some of my homework at home, my parents will help if I ask. Teachers will try to give me structured rather than open-ended tasks.	Record sheet of what I have done Homework will be in my books	

Table 1: Example of homework goal-setting support.

Teaching staff checklist

- Give the student enough time to write down homework.
- If the student with ASC can't write it clearly quickly enough, print it out on a piece of paper to stick in their book or allow the TA to write it for them. If the school uses

an online homework diary, check the student knows how to access it and speak to parents so that they can access it confidently too.

- Check with the student that they understand what they have to do. Ask '*Tell me what you have to do*' rather than '*Do you understand?*'. (Some students will say '*Yes*' to get you off their backs!)
- Tell the student exactly what is expected, how much they have to write and how long they should spend on it. Accept the work done in this time even if the task is not finished. Try to adjust tasks so that the student can complete it in a reasonable time. This will give you a clearer indication of how much they can process and achieve in that time.
- Try to match the homework task to the student's cognitive style. For example, if they are a visual learner, allow them to present their homework research in pictures, diagrams and flow charts. Writing frames also help by splitting the task into smaller chunks which can be looked at individually and provide natural breaks.
- Make use of learning support early on, before homework becomes too big a problem.
- If there is a plan or targets set to work up to doing homework then read it and work to them. Celebrate and praise the student's achievements of these goals.
- Try to structure tasks so that they are not too open-ended at first. Explain the outcome and give fewer options at first.
- Hold back on giving detentions. Providing homework support is far more successful than adding the stress of more time at school as a punishment.

What the SENCO or Head of Year can do

- Write a homework support plan with the parents and student. Get all to agree what they will do to help the student achieve homework success and what they can do if they are struggling. (**See the CD-ROM for a homework support plan template.**)
- Consider where in school time homework could be done. With students who require a lot of support, a reduced timetable with study periods to do homework and catch up on course work can be very successful.
- Be flexible and generous but track what homework is done and how well. An overview can identify difficulties with particular subjects or types of homework.
- Set up an email system with parents. This may enable you to track which subjects are causing the most stress for the student.
- Make consequences proportionate to the child's level of difficulty and explain what a detention is, how long it will last, and what they will do when they are there (e.g. '*Complete the unfinished homework*').
- Teach organisational skills and work with parents to help the student learn how to implement these at home. The aim should be to teach the student how to organise and manage their own study time eventually.
- Give the child a homework folder. This can just be a cardboard folder, checked each day by the student's teacher, TA and parent, with homework diary, paper hand-outs and even letters home in it. This keeps homework tasks together in the student's bag. Completed homework can be put in the folder to be found easily in lessons.

What parents can do

▸ Make a homework routine. This will work best if the student has some choices to make so that they feel they have ownership of the plan. Decide a time to rest, do homework and have screen time. Include tea and bedtime on the list, or if necessary make it into a visual timetable. Be clear about how long the homework or study time will be and have a reward activity on the timetable or list for after homework.

Fig. 3: A homework routine visual chart.

▸ You do not need to call it *'homework'*. Some people prefer to use the term *'study time'* which may also help when the student is in Year 10 and Year 11, having to do personal study for exam revision.

▸ Prepare the environment. Find a place in the home that is calm but not isolated, somewhere you can be around to help but not need to be sat next to them all the way through, and where siblings (especially younger ones) cannot demand attention, distract or destroy the work your child is doing. Turn the TV and other screens off or sit your child where they cannot directly see them. Have a drawer for them to put their school books in where they can always be found and have a spare set of pens and stationery in there. This works much better than their bedroom floor!

▸ Teach your child to organise themselves through writing lists. Write what has to be done each evening, spread it into chunks of 20–30 minutes (or 40–50 minutes if an older child) with regular 10-minute breaks. Give your child access to a list of break choices that do not include computer time or favourite toys as they will not want to come back to their homework. Try sensory breaks such as a drink of water, a run up and down the stairs, stretches, listening to music or a walk around the garden. Use a kitchen timer if that helps so that the alarm signifies when the break is due.

▸ Give praise that is specific. Don't underestimate the place of praise that tells your child exactly what they have done well. Rather than say *'You did well'* it can be more constructive to say things such as, *'You planned your work well tonight'*, *'You remembered your breaks and it has helped you complete all your work'* or *'You have tried really hard to concentrate'*.

▸ Be firm about screen time. This is very difficult but allowing your child to have a time to relax as soon as they come home can be essential. However, if they then refuse to come away from the computer, tablet or games console and homework is a battleground, then the screen time may need to be offered only once the homework time has been completed.

Teaching study and organisational skills

It is important for a student with ASC to learn how to do homework and study with as much independence as they can learn. If they are to achieve their full potential in achieving GCSEs and A Levels or other further study, then teaching them 'how to' rather than doing things for them will be important. Some students will require support throughout their secondary school life whereas others will become more independent.

There are some skills that can be taught that help with many aspects of school work and particularly with homework and independent study.

- **Self-motivation**

    Why do we do what we do? Usually it is for some form of gratification. Students with ASC may not be able to grasp the delayed gratification of earning school merits, pleasing the teacher or achieving good grades. Therefore, we can teach them to earn their own smaller, more regular and immediate rewards for completing homework tasks. At first they can work for 10 minutes or so and learn to tell themselves 'Well done me!' or put a star on a chart. When the full amount of work has been completed they can learn to give themselves praise and say what they did well: '*Yeah! I got to the end of the page*' or '*I asked for help with that!*'. A star translated into slots of time on the computer or game console can also be a self-motivating skill. I'm sure most adults apply this skill to an onerous task: have you ever worked for a bar of chocolate, a glass of wine or the end-of-month pay bonus?

- **Prioritising**

    This is a life skill that may need to be taught very intensely at first but with practice the student with ASC may be able to learn to prioritise more as they go through secondary schooling. Colour-coding can help. First the tasks will need to be examined and a code identified. You are aiming to teach the student how to decide what should be done first, what is most important and how they can time-manage the tasks so that each gets done on time. You may use red, yellow and green to prioritise but if they use traffic light colours for other systems, such as behaviour, I would suggest using other colours. You can also use the vocabulary of ordering, *First, Then, Next* and *Finally* and use a visual calendar to write when homework is due. This can be consulted each day and a priority list can be drawn from that.

- **Chunking**

    Show the student with ASC how to break a task into smaller chunks. One way is to give them a writing frame where the task is already split into smaller chunks, otherwise they can be supported to draw boxes around sections of the worksheet or task to break it up. Coloured felt-tip pens can help a visual learner, for example, do the red box first, then the blue box. This is particularly useful when they learn to do exams.

- **Creating a workspace**

    Understanding the conditions in which they work best can help a student with ASC organise the space they work in much better. They need to be aware of aspects such as their learning style, sensory triggers and what helps them stay focused. They need to acknowledge the distractions and what they would prefer to be doing. The workstation idea from TEACCH® can be set up in a student's bedroom or quiet corner of a living room. If they work well with a favourite item beside them or a fidget toy, then let them use this.

▶ Asking for help

A student with ASC can find frustration and the fear of failure a major barrier to being able to do homework. You can teach them to ask for help and when this is appropriate. A visual reminder can help with this. Use visuals to support the story, such as timelines, sequence of pictures, picture character maps, word banks that explain phrases, metaphors and idioms. Teaching *'What do I do if I think I can't do it?'* can help them overcome the situation where an hour is wasted becoming stressed and refusing to do what could be a 10-minute task. This can also be extended to helping them learn to ask the right questions when they are stuck. Rather than relying on an adult to tell them the answer they can be asked questions such as, *'What do you know about this?'*, *'Can you give me an example?'* or *'What part does make sense to you?'*.

▶ Mapping and planning

Mind maps or bullet-point planning are a good way to gather all the ideas together for a piece of work. They are visual ways of collecting thoughts and linking things together and can be particularly helpful in planning extended writing tasks. A bullet list of all the points that need to be covered or a mind map of all the ideas for a story can help a student with ASC keep on task and be able to see how all the information is included or linked together.

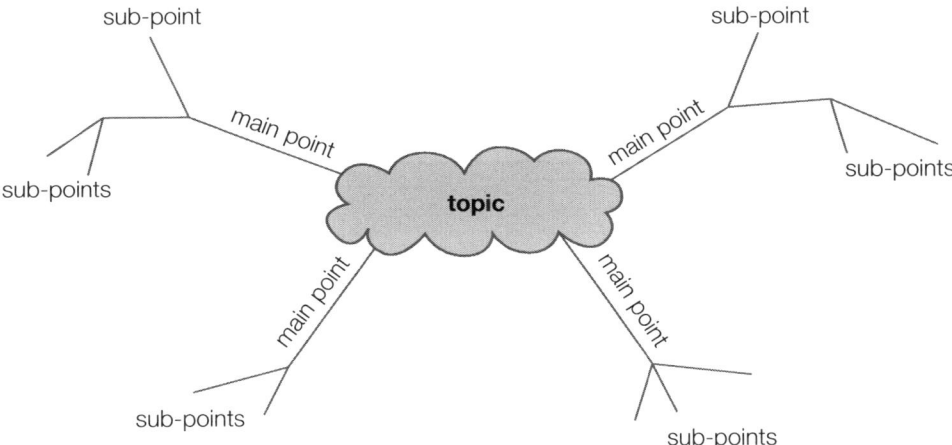

Fig. 4: A mind map diagram.

When all of the above is unsuccessful

"If all these strategies are unsuccessful, what is the alternative? Should children with an autistic spectrum disorder be exempted from doing homework? If the strategies outlined in this article are unsuccessful or unable to be implemented, then my reply is, 'Yes'. Sometimes this advice is to the great relief of the child, their parent and probably their teacher. You can quote me on this."

Tony Attwood (2000)

Some students with ASC may find trying to do homework so stressful that it leads to high levels of anxiety, overload and meltdowns. It is important to take things very slowly with a student experiencing this level of distress. The impact on their schooling, behaviour and mental health may be more than insisting on doing homework is worth. In these cases a much longer-term support strategy needs to be adopted. The student may need some time with no homework demands at all, and the emphasis of support being targeted instead at the student coping with the demands of the classwork and non-structured times. This is choosing your priorities carefully. Once the student has become more able to cope in school then homework can be introduced gently and gradually in carefully managed steps. Each step needs to be successful for the student and can build up to independent working.

Most students with ASC can learn to do homework if they are supported well. It is important to realise that there will be a few whose anxieties, poor organisation and other needs are too great for them to learn to work independently or cope with homework. They will need a differentiated approach which still enables them to achieve academically, such as doing tasks that are highly structured with TA support in school time. This may also need to be the approach to any course work they may have to do.

All the student's teachers need to be consistent in their support of homework, which can be one of the most difficult aspects of secondary school.

CHAPTER 6
Social communication and interaction

"School was a torture ground in itself for me because of my lack of social skills and my absolute terror of people (in part because I didn't just automatically know the social rules, and when I did learn them, I had to think about them all the time – and who can keep up that sort of coping skill ALL THE TIME?)."

Karen (*Martian in the Playground: Understanding the Schoolchild with Asperger's Syndrome*, 2000)

Secondary school is a huge social minefield for students with ASC. The demands to interact with others from the moment they approach the school gates, through tutor group, lessons with different teachers, break times and travelling on the bus, is constant and there are many overwhelming challenges to contend with.

"What these kids are missing is the script of life. Their biggest problem is knowing what's expected of them. You may look at this kid and think, 'He's smart; he should know better.' Well, he doesn't. It's not enough to tell him that what he's doing is wrong. You need to tell him what's right, going step by step."

Hoffmann-Zak (2007)

Students with ASC have a social impairment which is at the core of their diagnosis. Their brains struggle with processing social information. Observing what is happening, extracting the important information from what they see, interpreting it and knowing the appropriate response can be beyond most young people, and indeed adults with ASC. Learning a social language is twice as difficult as learning a second language says Tony Attwood (2008).

In neurotypical students they do all this unconsciously most of the time and can react almost instantly to a situation. Of course, all students growing and changing through puberty have times they are socially awkward, but in ASC there is a naivety and lack of awareness or understanding that goes beyond what is typical. There can be difficulty with:

- **Social interaction**
  This includes understanding what is happening in context, knowing how to respond, and taking other people's feeling and viewpoints into account. Not knowing how to interact socially can make it very hard to form friendships.

▷ **Social communication**

This includes understanding what is being communicated not only in words but non-verbally in gestures, facial expressions, tone of voice and context. It involves recognising when someone is being sarcastic, joking or teasing you. Students with ASC are hindered by their literal understanding and lack of ability to 'read' non-verbal communication. Social communication is also being able to join in conversations, know what topics people might like to talk about, and follow the flow of a one-to-one or group conversation.

▷ **Social imagination**

This includes the ability to understand and predict other people's intentions and behaviour and to imagine situations outside of their own regular experiences. This may be accompanied by a narrow repetitive range of activities, obsessions and dominating a conversation or activity.

"The teachers don't realise I don't mean to be rude. It's just that I can't tell what tone my voice is speaking in. And frankly, I know a lot and when they get something wrong I'm only correcting them. But I'm the one shouted at for telling them the truth."
Boy with ASC, Year 8

Tony Attwood considers that there are three types of social characters in autism. The first is **introverted, isolated** and **withdrawn**. In secondary schools they will be the students hanging around the fringes of the outside area, being late to lessons because they have taken the long way round and who would rather do anything than sit with or work with others. They feel much safer avoiding people and can be very vulnerable to being bullied. They are often highly anxious.

The second are **intrusive, intense** and **abrasive**. They don't read the signals to understand when to draw the line and are often in conflict with others through arguments and fighting. They want to be in the middle of a crowd, the centre of attention and want to be in control of what the group does. They do not like it when others make suggestions and can become angry, abusive or violent if things don't go their way. You will notice that most of their interactions and friendships are one way or based on intense common interests. They may be loud and brash and take lots of risks with words and actions because they lack the social skills to have proper conversations and more mature interactions.

The third are those who **observe, analyse** and **imitate** and many of this group will be girls with ASC. They don't understand social situations intuitively but have developed an enormous capacity to copy what others are doing. In primary schools this has often been enough for them to get by, but with the increasing complexity of social relationships and interests in the secondary school years, these students will start to seem awkward and out of place even in their friendship groups. They may be increasingly left out and not know why or become the butt of teasing. Their imitating behaviour may become obsessive. They may copy another person's mannerisms, clothing and interests and can be perceived as obsessional.

It is clear that social interaction causes the most stress, anxiety, anger and conflict in students with ASC. There are many skills needed to be able to interact successfully with others and these become more complex as the students go through their teenage years and into adulthood. The need to negotiate a variety of relationships is vital to be able to function in adult life. A student with an Education, Health and Care (EHC) Plan will have a social interaction support requirement set out in their plan, however for others it is important that key staff at secondary school look to provide support to build up the skills and confidence in social interaction of students with ASC in order to fully meet their needs. A structured, personalised programme to address the student's needs throughout their years at secondary school is essential.

It is important to respect the student's wishes and remember that we are not forcing them to be like 'everyone else', or giving them a set of rigid 'rules' of how to behave around others. No … the student with ASC needs to be able to have skills and coping strategies to enable them to deal with other people, in different situations, have successful friendships and relationships and to know how to keep themselves safe from being exploited and bullied, whilst knowing that who they are and being autistic is entirely acceptable. We must respect their desires not to get involved or to withdraw and teach them that this is okay too.

Friendships

It is a myth that students with ASC don't want friends. It may be that some students are happy with their own company and other people are just too confusing and stressful to be with and this should be respected. However, many more people with ASC do want to have friendships but find themselves often without friends. Not only do their social communication impairments cause difficulties, but often, other students are a barrier to the student with ASC having friends. Other students' reactions to their interests, behaviours and differences can be negative, teasing and often cruel. The fear, anger and sadness that results can cause the person with ASC to become more aggressive or withdrawn, so the isolation and loneliness increases. This is far too common an experience for students with ASC in many secondary schools.

> *"I usually follow a group of girls around because I want them to be my friend. They often laugh at things I don't understand and I laugh along just to be included. I suspect that sometimes they are laughing at me but I don't want to complain in case they say they don't want to be my friend. I invited them all to my birthday party but none of them came."*
>
> Girl with ASC, Year 10

The social naivety of students with ASC can make them vulnerable to being made fun of, taken advantage of and being bullied by others who they think are their friends. This can even lead to 'mate crime' in that they are dared or persuaded to break the rules, steal or give their own money to their 'mates' who have realised that they are an easy target, desperate for friendship. This destructive pattern of relationships can continue into adulthood.

Conversely, the benefits of genuine friendships are that peers are better role models for social situations and understanding than adults.

A peer friendship can help a student with ASC learn how to act in different situations and how to deal with conflict or unsafe situations, usually when no adult is present. Try looking for a peer from the student's own year group. A peer who shares the same interests and sense of humour with a student with ASC can make a great difference to break times and lunchtimes. They may introduce the student to a wider circle of friends and be able to guide them away from stressful situations or potential danger. They can remind them of their calming strategies when they are feeling angry and teach them how to understand jokes and teasing. As with all people, a good friend provides comfort and hope when things do go wrong – as they sometimes will. They affirm you and encourage you. A student with ASC can be a good, loyal and fun friend.

Try giving the student with ASC the opportunity to find real peers of all ages through special interest groups and clubs within the school. Be creative in what they can try and prepare the student (remembering they do not usually like change or new situations and so will need more support than other students to try something new) through pre-visits, photos, exploring websites, asking leaders to come to school to talk about what they do, giving the student a particular project to do.

Students with ASC could try:

Lunchtime and after-school clubs

Setting up lunchtime and after-school clubs that cover the student's special interests can be a good way to foster friendships. This does not always need staff expertise (only supervision) as the students can also learn to take on roles of responsibility and learn leadership and co-operation skills in setting up and running a club. Some schools have successfully done this with a common interest such as Minecraft, and students have worked together making tutorials for younger children.

Snack and chat

Making sure there is access to quiet places and areas during break and lunchtimes so that students can meet with others without the busyness of the school outside area. One school set up a 'Snack and chat' session each lunchtime in a classroom, supervised by a member of staff. It gave students with ASC and other needs the environment to chat and get to know others and with support, develop the skills to engage in social conversations and activities with others.

Buddy system

Younger students with ASC can be set up with a 'buddy' (a student in the same year or an older student). They may also have ASC or be a student who has the aptitude to gain an understanding of ASC and how it may affect the student. Finding buddies may need to rely on staff knowledge of other students to invite them, or be a more formal scheme that students sign up to. It is important that buddies are a good match and the student with ASC does like them. If they have good social skills, are reliable, have a positive attitude to the role and have the perseverance to stay with the role for at least a whole school year or beyond, they should be able to develop a good balanced relationship with their buddy. There are many young people who, given the support, could become good friends and advocates for students with ASC in your school. The buddy system is usually monitored and students meet regularly to talk over any issues with a member of staff. This includes the student with ASC, as it is something done with them, not for them. Training is given to all the students (including those students with ASC) about how to be good friends. This system can benefit all the students involved and has led some students on to careers such as teaching because of the opportunities it gave them to learn about supporting others.

Jones, V (2007) stated that students involved in buddying students with ASC and other special needs were, on the whole, very positive and enthusiastic about their experiences and felt that they had learned much they could take with them into their adult life, as well as making a friends they may not have previously considered. Students with ASC say these friendships have made the difference to them being happy and liked in school. They have enjoyed being a good friend to their buddy too.

> **Important considerations**
>
> When talking to peer buddies it is important to first establish boundaries and a culture of respect. The student with ASC is not a 'patient' or a 'project' and other students should not be given any power over a student with ASC, such as being able to tell them what they *must* do. Friendship is a two-way interaction and mutual respect and trust must be part of it. Teachers cannot engineer that, only support it. It may not be necessary for the buddy to know about ASC, but if it is, then the student with ASC should be able to choose what information is shared. If a school has an inclusive ethos, where all students with disabilities are seen as able and included, where teasing because of difference is not tolerated, and kindness, respect and belonging to a community is encouraged, then it is more likely that students will have positive attitudes to those who have ASC and other differences.

Social skills group

Set up a regular social skills group where students with ASC can learn about the skills they need to approach others, have good conversations, read body language and social situations through context and how to recognise who they can trust and who they shouldn't. Do this through fun activities and games where possible.

Community activities

Encourage and enable students with ASC to get involved in community activities. Many schools have eco-committees, support charities or put on special events. A student with ASC could have a role to play even if it is a 'back-stage' role. Church schools often have strong links that could be harnessed.

There are clubs and all kinds of activities in most communities that a student with ASC could access. Parents can be encouraged to get them involved in activities, clubs and events in and outside school, such as:

Sports

Some sports are not team based and so might be more appealing, such as karate, trampolining, freerunning, rock climbing.

Scouts and cadets

Scouts and cadets are usually well structured and have activities in which new skills are learned.

Music

If they are interested in music, students could join a community band, choir or drama group.

Charity work

Charities are always looking for volunteers and this is a good way for students to use their interests and to learn skills through helping others. Students can raise money through harnessing their special interests or organising a display or event in school with others.

Special interest magazines are a good source of ideas. It is good for a student with ASC to meet people of all ages and it can develop their skills and confidence if they spend time mixing with others in and out of school. The organisation may need ASC training and local charities or the National Autistic Society can often help with this. The student can learn many life skills, have an outlet for their energy and a place where they build friendships for life.

"When I was in my teens I found it hard to make friends, not because no one wanted to be friends but because I could not tell they wanted to be."

Paddy-Joe Moran, adult with Asperger's

Assessing social skills

There is no exact science in assessing a student with ASC and their social interaction ability. There are various checklists in books and online that can be used to give a picture of the strengths and weaknesses of the student with ASC. However, it is useful that a SENCO or mentor has a fuller picture of the student's ability and difficulties through observation and discussion with the student, not as a definitive list of 'can and can'ts', but as a baseline from which to work from and record progress. The sooner this is done, for example over the first term of Year 7, the sooner a personalised programme can be planned and put in place. In this assessment it is important to involve the student themselves and to interview their parents wherever possible. You are aiming to build up a picture of the student's interests, communication abilities, receptive and cognitive understanding of communication and their ability to read social situations accurately. The questions should include information about awareness of others, ability to comment, join in and approach others. It should look at how they approach conversations, understanding of inference, sarcasm, jokes and teasing and what makes them upset, confused or angry. It should note the student's interests and successful attempts at interacting with others and look for situations that they feel comfortable in or particularly enjoy. (**See the social skills checklist on the CD-ROM.**)

Students with ASC should always be included in their own target setting when planning what social skills they should be taught. A good way is to let them assess their own skills and then say what they would like to achieve. Often these targets may seem a long way off where they are, and then a visual scale can be helpful to show the student how they can work towards their goal. One student I worked with was keen to be able to be able to talk to others about different topics that interested them but then said *'But I'll never be able to do that!'*. We broke down the target into smaller steps where he learned a bit more about how to have conversations, practised the skills in our group and then gave him tasks to do each week, such as listen to what others are talking about and make a list of topics. Over a school year the student had moved himself from 2 on his scale to a 7 and felt much more confident in talking to others. (**See the my steps to success chart on the CD-ROM.**)

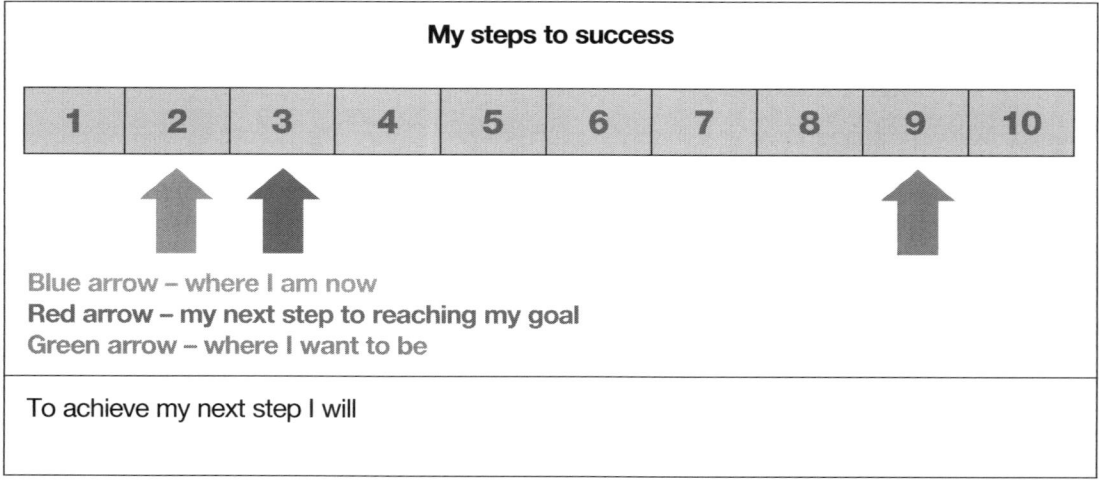

Fig. 5: Steps to success chart.

Developing a social skills programme

Students with ASC benefit from a structured social skills programme throughout their years at secondary school. A social skills programme should be structured but flexible, taught, experienced, practised and allow the student to have ownership and a chance to evaluate their own learning and development. Using the 10-point scale can be a good way of involving the students with their own target setting and progress monitoring. However, teaching a social skills programme needs flexibility from the school. Time in the student's timetable will need to be allowed for these sessions and a mixture of group work and individual work can be needed. These sessions will need to be regular and provide opportunities for generalising the skills taught in the regular classrooms and unstructured times. Often the SENCO or a TA may lead these sessions, or a school may buy in a specialist teacher to do so. Some schools may run these sessions in assembly time, break times, lunchtimes or off-timetable, depending on the needs of the students.

The PSHE curriculum may be a guide but does not cover the issues in the depth and breadth many students with ASC need. For many students with ASC the PSHE curriculum in Key Stages 3 and 4 is too abstract or they are in danger of misunderstanding, taking things literally or being unable to accept other points of view and opinions. There are many good commercial resources on the market, such as *Socially Speaking* by Alison Schroeder or the *Talkbout* series by Alex Kelly, which provide structured teaching plans, resources and group activity ideas that are practical and relevant. It is a good idea to choose at least two programmes and personalise them to your students. It is important to be flexible so that issues raised by the students can be explored in the next session, rather than left for a long time. When choosing a commercial programme it is good to look for photocopiable resources, clear and chunked information and visuals to support the concepts and learning – or you could make your own.

Students with ASC can be taught about skills and then given the opportunity to look for examples and to practise these skills. It is important to build in self-awareness and self-esteem, for students to understand their ASC and that it is not 'wrong', but a difference. The sessions should be driven by the students working out what areas they find difficult and wanting to find a way to make it easier for them.

To start – building on the basics

Students with ASC have an uneven development in their social understanding and skills. They may have not yet developed some important foundational social skills and the nature of ASC is that some students will not develop all of the skills they need through into adulthood. Eye contact, for example, may be a difficulty for them throughout their life. Understanding small-talk or chatting may never make sense to them, and approaching others may always be the most uncomfortable and stressful thing they do in their lives. We need to keep this in mind as we go through a social skills programme and allow the students to learn at their own pace and give them the means by which to express their own views and difficulties about the skills we are discussing. A structured approach and explaining to the students what the skills are can be a good way to encourage their self-awareness and learning.

I often encourage schools to begin with a few basic skills to teach, getting the students themselves to define what they are, how to use them and then to practise them in a safe and structured context first. Board and card games are a good way in for many students with ASC in learning social skills. They are not 'work' and if taught and structured well can provide lots of opportunity to practise the skills you are teaching. We often begin with five skills.

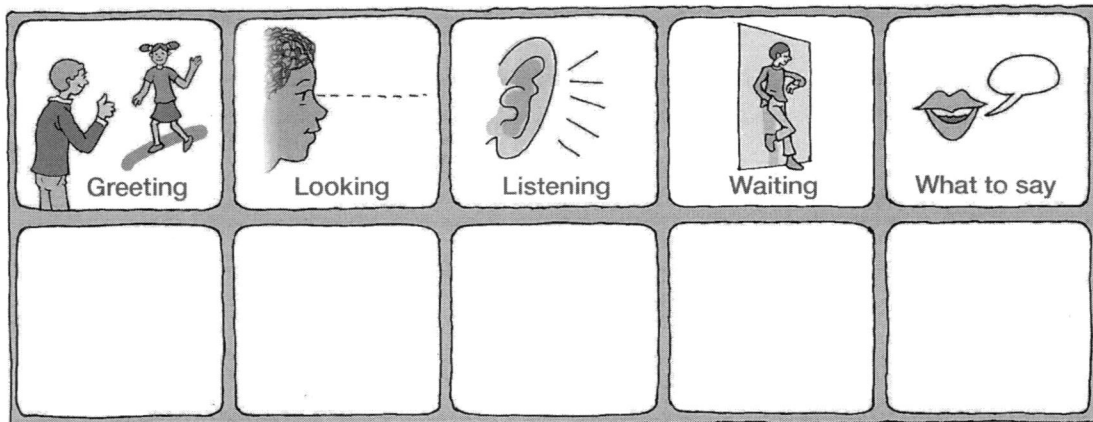

Fig. 6: Five social skills board.

The students in the group (which will include those with ASC but may also include students with good social skills and 'buddies') can write a definition of the skills and then play a board or card game where they can practise these skills. The teacher will give points to the students when they notice the skills being used and students will be encouraged to notice the skills in themselves and each other. The points are earned towards whatever reward the group decides, either individual or shared. By playing a variety of games over a few weeks and encouraging the students to practise these skills in their lessons you are encouraging generalisation of the skills. Some students may collect points from their subject teachers if this encourages them and the teachers have been briefed. These five skills can be a focus of a whole term's group work until the students feel confident.

Moving on – conversation skills

Conversations are all around us and students with ASC may have difficulty starting a conversation, joining in or knowing how to end it. They may not be able to tell when someone is bored, or teasing, or being sarcastic. They may interrupt or want to talk about their interests and opinions all the time. Again, showing how a conversation can be structured, the kinds of topics that different people discuss and how to start, end and continue can be useful skills for all students. Students with ASC don't always understand that a conversation is a sharing of ideas and opinions and that you can disagree without arguing or destroying a friendship. In a structured session it is a good idea to begin with a definition of what a conversation is and how it works. There are some good conversation skill resources in the *Talkabout* series of books and www.do2learn.com have good conversation-related Social Stories™ to download for free.

Students may need to do some work about how to start a conversation, asking and answering questions and what type of questions can be good to ask in a conversation. Topic cards can be used to help students choose what to start talking about. The more the students with ASC make suggestions and give their own ideas, the more they will be able to develop their own understanding of social communication. It is important to teach 'how to leave a conversation politely' for situations where they feel under pressure, overloaded and uncomfortable.

Working on conversations can be done over the whole of a school year and be refreshed over the following school years. I have worked with students on this topic regularly from Year 7 through to Year 11 as we discuss the increasing development of conversations and who they might need to talk to in their experiences. It has led to more confidence for interviews and moving on to college for older students who have had a lot of support on this in earlier years.

Next steps – being a 'social detective'

It is important to teach students with ASC that there are no definite 'right' or 'wrong' answers. Social 'reading' is like being a detective or scientist; the 'reader' is looking for evidence and clues. They then make a 'good guess' based on the evidence and clues as to what the other person is thinking, intending or means. It may always be a difficult concept for students with ASC but they can learn to understand social situations a little better with a great deal of practice. It introduces the important concept of **context.** Whereas neurotypical students have a natural capacity to make good guesses about what is happening in a social sense (and they sometimes get it wrong too), the student with ASC will have to work hard at this. Good friends and peers can be invaluable in helping them with this and some neurotypical peers in the group can be useful, as long as they do not dominate the discussions. With many students they may respond to it as a game or challenge. This is a visual I have created to help with this concept. (**See the social detective visual on the CD-ROM.**)

Fig. 7: A 'social detective' sign.

The aspects of social communication students with ASC could learn about include:

- **'reading people'** using facial expressions, body language and posture. What are people telling us non-verbally? How do we guess their intentions?
- **emotions** – how do people display these? What are appropriate responses?
- **non-literal language** such as sarcasm, humour and jokes, inference, slang and idioms
- **context** – what is happening around the incident, what are the context clues?
- **tone of voice**, intonation, pitch and volume of speech and how people interpret those
- **different types of questions** and which are most useful and when

- **manners, assertiveness, arguments and communication breakdowns** – how do we know people are bored or want to leave the conversation?
- **social media etiquette** – how much is too much?; learning to take time to understand clues before replying, knowing when to ignore
- **trust and keeping safe** – how to get out of uncomfortable or threatening situations (including online)
- **character** – how do we assess someone's character from the way they behave?
- **different types of consequences** – positive as well as negative
- what are people's **rights and responsibilities** to each other?
- how do we look after our **mental health** and how can others help us?

As you can see, there is enough in this list to keep going from Year 7 to Year 11. You can use many techniques to teach these skills including:

- visual pictures of real life situations
- social stories™
- video clips
- role-play
- games
- problem-solving activities
- projects to work on alone or with a partner or as a group
- mapping ideas out to see the connections
- puppets.

Teaching students about their ASC

"My parents told me I was autistic. I thought it meant that I was going to die. It made my behaviour awful at school because I was so scared. It got much better when my specialist teacher helped me understand my autism. I'm still a bit scared but not because I think I'll die any time soon."

Boy with ASC, Year 7

Some students with ASC know a lot about their condition. They may be keen to talk about it and share their knowledge with their peers. Some may have a little knowledge, knowing that they have a diagnosis but it has not been explained to them in a way that they can relate to. Other students may have not been told they have a condition called ASC and may be confused and frustrated about why they are having special interventions and support in school.

It is important that any discussion about a student's condition or diagnosis is done in partnership with parents and a specialist ASC teacher or service. This can be done in school or by outside agencies. It is important for the student to explore their strengths, not just their difficulties, and for those talking to them about their diagnosis to be aware that no two people with ASC are the same while the student needs to be able to understand ASC in the way that it affects them personally.

For all students with ASC their condition is pervasive: it affects every part of who they are and their lives. Some of those effects will be personal and private. It is important not to push the boundaries of personal information and expect the student with ASC to give us more information than we would expect from their peers, unless it is they who want to share it with us. As with all students, safeguarding and professional boundaries must be kept at the forefront at all times. We must also remember that they are children and then teenagers, and like all other students in the school are grappling with puberty, identity, developing opinions and preferences during these formative years. Their autism will change and develop with them, too, therefore we should not be speaking about absolutes, but about experiences and learning. If you are in doubt about whether to, or how to, talk about their autism, ask the student first, and seek specialist help.

CHAPTER 7
Tests and examinations

Tests and exams are part of school life. Students with ASC will have already experienced SATs (Standard Assessment Tests) before they start secondary school and for some they will have managed these with support, for others they will have been highly stressful or even traumatic. Some may have been unable to sit these exams.

In the first few weeks of Year 7 many schools do CATs (Cognitive Abilities Tests). Some students with ASC may cope with these better as they are online and can be treated as a normal ICT lesson activity.

Our education system is set up to test neurotypical children and can fail to assess the learning of students with ASC adequately. The way they think about and process information, have their own priorities and creativity is different and their development progression is often uneven, not particularly following typical development patterns. They often are unable to understand implied meaning (particularly when answering exam questions) which can cause tests and exams to be a major source of stress and mental health issues. Some students with ASC become obsessed with the importance of the test or exam and cannot cope with the thought that they may fail or get a poor mark. This can lead to them refusing to take the test at all. Others cannot work out how to do a test, especially when their usual support may not be able to help in the same way. They focus on questions they know about, write everything they know about it, but then answer none of the other questions. For example, a Year 10 boy doing a science exam found his TA could read the questions to him but couldn't explain what they meant. He answered many of his questions literally and received a score far less than his actual knowledge reflected.

We have a system we must work within, for now, and the best advice is to prepare students with ASC as early as possible, whilst early identification of those for whom you will need to apply for exam concessions is very important. Even very bright students with ASC may need exam concessions such as more time or a reader, and you will need to build up the evidence for this early on. Getting parents on-board and working with them will be very important and the anxiety about tests and exams is felt as much by them as their child. The stress and anxiety is often displayed more at home than at school and working with parents and taking note of what they say can make a major difference to the student's support and success.

Class-based tests

It is a good idea to explain to the student that class tests are part of what they do in school, and the reason for them. Students with ASC like to know the reason and purpose for things. This can be done through a Social Story™. (**For an example, see I can do a test! social story on the CD-ROM.**)

It may help to begin with tests that are narrow in focus and short, which have more chance of the student getting a good score. As with most things, early success is important: would you be keen to keep doing something you usually did badly at? It is also important to have high expectations and plan to increase the amount and content the student is able to cope with in a test. This must not be done in a way that only increases the student's anxiety. This would work well as a whole-school approach so that the student learns success in tests in all their subjects. You could:

- use a separate room
- include short breaks
- do the test over two days
- cover up all questions but the one they are working on (e.g. by using pieces of paper to cover the other questions; folding the paper; or using a window cut of a piece of card)
- use a sand timer to help them know how much time to give to each question.

Case study

A Year 8 student with ASC refused to do a talk to his class. He was so anxious about it that he was not sleeping and started to refuse to come to school. The English teacher sat with him to make a plan. She knew he was interested in Lego® and asked him if he could put some information about Lego® together to teach others something about it. He agreed that he would like to do that. They also agreed that he would tell this information to a TA he was working with, in a quiet room with just her as the audience. The boy prepared his talk and a PowerPoint presentation to go with it. When the day came he was happy to be talking about his favourite topic and proud of what he had prepared. But then disaster struck as his presentation had not loaded onto his data pen and the student almost went into meltdown. However, without a class audience, his TA was able to help him calm down enough to find a picture on the computer and deliver the talk. He presented very well, answered questions and was able to receive a good grade. It may have taken some time, but this student now has a little confidence and success that he can take into the next talk he has to do. He may never talk in front of the whole class but may be able to aim for a small group of trusted friends to present to.

Exam concessions

It is important to assess and apply early in Year 10 for any access arrangements for students with ASC who will be sitting GCSE exams at the end of Year 11. The Joint Council for Qualifications (JCQ) has all the information and guidance and it is the school's SENCO that usually takes responsibility for assessing and applying for special arrangements. It is useful for subject teachers to read this guidance so that they can provide accurate and supported information to the SENCO to support the assessment and application. The concessions available include access arrangements such as a reader and/or scribe, extra time, use of ICT and a separate venue to sit the exam. There are also applications for modified papers for students who have dyslexia, visual impairment and other conditions.

Revision support

Students with ASC often have poor organisation, sequencing, and literal and rigid thinking patterns which impact greatly on their ability to revise and prepare for exams. It is important to support them in planning their revision personally and not relying on the reams of advice given to all the students in the year. A bespoke revision plan can make all the difference. The student with ASC may need to know how long to spend revising, how to test themselves on what they know, when to have breaks, and support in understanding questions and the language of exam scripts. The more they understand what they are doing, how long it will take and what they can do to reduce anxiety, the more they will be able to cope with exams. Consider:

- sitting with the student and a blank timetable. Use sticky notes to write down all the revision that needs to be done and try out different ways of fitting it on the timetable. Make sure there are enough rest times and breaks where the student can reward themselves with favourite activities.
- making use of the many different revision activities online. Apps and BBC Bitesize can cover most of the revision a student needs which will appeal more to a student who likes being on their computer.
- talking about dealing with the worry about exams. Use strategies mentioned in Chapter 6 to explore how the student is feeling and what regulation strategies they can use. Make a visual reminder card to give them, including drinking water, taking a walk and other physical activities.
- reducing other pressures in school. Allow small things to be ignored (such as uniform misdemeanours) and build familiarity with the exam hall or room into the student's routine.
- instead of study leave, invite the student into school to revise with the learning support department or a small group of other students. They should know what access to subject teachers they have and have some be made available to go over things with them.
- practice, practice, practice – in small chunks to begin with so that the student gets used to the language of the exams and what questions mean. Spend time explaining the meaning of key phrases (e.g. *Can you explain...?* means you have to write an explanation, not just write *Yes*).

Exam-time stress

The days of the actual exams are stressful for all students but students with ASC, no matter how well prepared they have been, are more likely to have panic attacks and extreme anxiety that may prevent them from doing well in the exam, or even doing it at all. Where possible the school could help by inviting the student into school earlier, walking them through the exam room, talking them through the exam and relaxation techniques they use and reassuring them of their ability.

We can all remind students that exams are not going to ruin their lives. Schools must teach students with ASC that there are more chances, more learning and more opportunities after and outside school. Schools must teach that students' strengths can lead to a career and help them see that there are jobs that they can do where they can use and develop their interests. Exam stress is often compounded by transition stress and some of the strategies for Key Stages 4–5 in Chapter 13 can help.

CHAPTER 8
Supporting behaviour

"Behaviour in ways that others identify as 'challenging' or problematic is not exclusive to people with autism. It is part of being human. Most of our behaviours reflect attempts to meet our needs, satisfy our desires, cope with frustrations and high levels of emotion."

Clements & Zarkowska (2000)

Students with ASC can have the same variety of behaviours as all students in a secondary school. Some follow all the rules, are keen to please the teacher and have impeccable manners. Others may seem to be engaged in low-level disruptive behaviours which annoy and distract the teachers and other students. Some engage in repetitive behaviours that are self-stimulating but are seen as odd or annoying to others. Yet others display destructive, obstinate, refusal, challenging and harmful behaviours that impact on themselves and others, disrupting everyone's learning. Some find the behaviour of other students unpredictable, confusing and stressful and may be 'on pins' all through the school day and then seem to overreact to small and seemingly unimportant events, especially other students 'winding them up'.

We can understand any disruptive or challenging behaviours through the lens of the student's ASC. Their behaviours need to be 'read' correctly. Teachers need to be asking what the behaviour is communicating rather than immediately assuming that the student is being naughty or doing it on purpose. Many books about ASC and behaviour (Cumine et al, 2009; Moyes, 2013; Brown, 2015) explain that the behaviour we see is only the visible demonstration of underlying issues and conditions. Cumine et al explain this as 'the iceberg of behaviour'. What we see above the surface is only a fraction of the mass underneath the surface. It is also important to understand that students with ASC who manage to 'keep it all together' at school all day can easily have daily meltdowns and rages as soon as they get home. Having good behaviour at school does not mean the student with ASC does not have significant challenges because of their ASC throughout every school day.

> *Imagine the student with ASC is like a bottle of fizzy pop. Events, stresses and demands throughout the day are like the fizzy pop being shaken up, but the student manages to just about keep the lid on. This may take them an awful lot of effort, just to 'keep it together' in the school day. What is common is that the student gets home and they can no longer keep the lid on the fizzy pop bottle and it explodes…along with the contents. That's why parents often say their child has a meltdown when they get home from school. (And then can't get them to do their homework).*

As we have already discussed, ASC is a communication, social, sensory and flexible thinking difference. The majority of students with ASC do not have challenging behaviour. However, when they do, a student's inappropriate and challenging behaviour could be for any number of reasons. The issue is that it displays in your classrooms as wilful disobedience and distraction. The student may be refusing or just not getting on with their work. They may call out, talk over others or become distressed and argumentative. They may sit too close to others, be unable to work in a group, complain at others, take things that are not theirs, not follow your instructions, bang their head on the table, fiddle with something or make constant noises. They may become very angry, hit out at others, throw things, shout and scream, hurt themselves and destroy equipment. They may refuse to move, run away, threaten others or have a total meltdown. They might tell lies, or always say what they think, they might think they know more than the teacher and say so. They might refuse to do their homework, be in a complete panic about a test, refuse to go in a classroom because it smells different or you changed where they sit. They may never start or complete a piece of work without constant prompting and they may cry, wet themselves or become completely withdrawn. They can be depressed, overwhelmed and in a constant state of anxiety. Any child can have any behaviour if the circumstances lead them to it. ASC is no different, it's only the challenges the students have that give them more stress and anxiety. It is clear, then, that students with ASC need a supported approach to their behaviour.

Our first question should always be, 'What is making them anxious?'.
Then, 'What is it that they don't understand?'.

Across the secondary school it can be difficult to monitor behaviours and collect the data to analyse it, however, this is the most effective way to begin to understand and support positive and appropriate behaviours and reduce stress for the student. Your school may have a behaviour monitoring system that can be utilised and you can ask the student about their behaviour. It isn't just asking them '*Why?*' or to explain themselves, as many won't be able to; it is about asking them about the people, the environment, their perceptions and what they think are the triggers. It can be difficult for some students to express their thoughts but others may welcome the opportunity to talk about their anxieties.

School rules and classroom behaviour

Every secondary school has a student behaviour policy and a set of rules that students are expected to follow. Often these are printed in the front of the student's planner so that they are available to all students all the time. The majority of secondary schools have a clear discipline policy that is structured and sets out clearly what behaviour is unacceptable and what will happen at each stage of the discipline procedures. Where these are applied consistently they can bring comfort to students with ASC who like to keep the rules and make sure that others are keeping them too. As all students with ASC are different, their understanding and response to school rules will be different too. Most students do learn the rules and are keen to follow them and, as with all teenagers, may want to test them occasionally. What can happen is that the student with ASC doesn't understand the application of the rule, they may be quite sure that they have not broken a rule (which may be literally true), but our interpretation of their behaviour has caused a situation to occur. Incidents such as uniform transgressions, being rude to the teacher (when the student is only telling the truth but in a tone of voice that is interpreted as rude) and being late to class can often be blown out of proportion because the student has misunderstood or does not have the skills to do what would be expected in that situation. Conversely, some students with ASC are so afraid and anxious about breaking a rule that they can become stressed and upset at the slightest hint that a teacher might not be pleased with them.

> *"At first I couldn't remember all the rules, there were just too many, but my TA put some simpler ones in my planner and just explained them to me each day."*
> Girl with ASC, Year 7

This does not mean that the majority of students with ASC cannot follow the school behaviour policy and rules. It may mean that they may need some extra support to be able to apply the rules and to deal with the slight variations of expectation that occur between different teachers. Some ways that you can help could be:

- go through the rules and explain what each one means in practice. Don't do them all at once. Form tutors could look at one each day at the beginning of the year and then refer to them regularly.
- if they need it, consider giving a shorter version of the rules with visuals to put in the student with ASC's planner. (**See the rules visual on the CD-ROM.**)
- being aware that sanctions often cause more anxiety and stress than effective support for students with ASC. SENCOs should assess the right way to support a student and make a plan based on specialist teacher advice or using a functional behaviour analysis.
- ensure that any plan is implemented consistently by all subject teachers. Inconsistency is usually a huge factor in the breakdown of a mainstream placement.
- make sure the student with ASC knows why they have received the sanction and make the reason specific rather than general. You may need to explain which one of the rules they have violated.

If the student is motivated by the school reward system, ensure that they understand what they will receive and when. Some schools have these electronically stored and students need to log in to the system to see their points/rewards. Students with ASC may need a visual record they can have with them. This could be a printout each week with an update of their online record.

> *"I always liked rules, they helped me. But it really used to bug me when some teachers would let people talk when we were working and some would make us work in silence. I did get really angry at people making noise in some lessons."*
> Boy with ASC, Year 9

Classroom behaviour management for students with ASC

There are many strategies you can use that are positive and directive responses to behaviour rather than negative 'telling off' or punishments. These reward the student with positive teacher attention.

> *Brown (2015) suggests that, "Behaviour management interventions often come down to thinking ahead, being assertive and being confident.".*

I would also add that it involves consistency and perseverance – don't be too quick to say something isn't working as the student with ASC may need a lot of practice to adjust their behaviour. It is also important to remember that ASC is a disability which we have a responsibility to understand and meet the needs this causes the students to have (SEND Code of Practice 2015). Of course, if the other students in the lesson are behaving well, it helps the student with ASC have good role models.

Strategies that support students with ASC include:

- **redirecting** inappropriate behaviour by telling the student specifically what behaviour you do want (e.g. *'I want you to sit quietly and listen to what I'm telling you'* rather than *'Behave yourself'* or *'Stop doing that'*.)
- **distracting** the student from inappropriate behaviour by directing their focus onto their work and praising them for something they have achieved
- **giving choices** rather than direct confrontation (e.g. *'Do you want to sit quietly at your table or move to where you can work on your own?'*)
- **using special interests** to motivate the student. If their interest has no relevance to your subject or topic, motivate them with the chance to talk to you about it at the end of a lesson or build it into a reward scheme. One student loved taking apart old laptops and mobile phones. He was struggling to behave appropriately in some lessons and was given a reward card to earn time with a broken laptop and a screwdriver. This improved his behaviour in most subjects. If a topic is talked about when the student should be concentrating on the lesson, give them a visual reminder of the appropriate time to talk, such as break time.
- **reducing sensory input** by allowing the student to draw the blinds, wear headphones or let them choose where is most comfortable for them to sit
- **adjusting your language** to avoid the use of the word *'always'* as in *'We must always…'*. You are setting impossible standards that not even adults can keep. Use the word *'finish'* instead of *'stop'*; the words *'sometimes'* and *'usually'* instead of *'always'* and make sentences short so you can pause to give processing time. Say what you mean, clearly, without waffling or using sarcasm.
- **moving to stand beside the student** to speak to them rather than confronting them or standing over them. Use a neutral tone of voice.
- **staying positive** and in control of your emotions. Try to explain to the student what emotion you see them displaying (e.g. *'It looks like you are frustrated with not being able to answer those maths questions. I'm here to help you. Tell me what you are struggling with.'*).
- **reducing pressure** by giving them less work so that they are able to achieve. I'm sure we would rather have half a page they completed themselves than two pages completed by the TA.
- **not assuming that** students with ASC may not understand the impact their behaviour has on others. Explain objectively, not with accusation. Also let them explain the impact others' behaviour has on them.
- **keeping changes to a minimum** by explaining and warning students when changes will happen where possible and have a Social Story™ or written explanation of what to do if the teacher or room changes. Don't change your seating plan too often and allow a student with ASC to stay in the same place or near the same people.
- **labelling the behaviour, not the student**. It is important to say that you didn't like the behaviour, or it was the wrong thing to do, rather than imply in any way that the student themselves are 'wrong'. Be aware of a student's sensitivity to their diagnosis. (This is also helpful for students who try to use their diagnosis as an excuse for their behaviour.)
- **giving 'time out'** before things get too stressful; if you recognise that the student is 'brewing' then let them go out of class for a short while. This can be a safe place such

as learning support or the library, or just being allowed to stand in the corridor for an agreed time. You could also send the student on an errand to give them a break from the classroom. You may need a code between you and the student so they can ask for a break without it being obvious to others and agree how long it will last beforehand.

- **using simple visuals** that help a student with ASC remember what it is they are supposed to be doing. You can link it to their favourite characters, make it amusing and help them do the right thing, rather than being shouted at because they just can't remember what they should be doing when their brain is full of so many other things they are trying to work out.

> *"I wish they [teachers] would just tell me what I'd done wrong and what the consequence is, instead of waffling on about how good I have been doing before they get to the point. I know I do things wrong, I can accept there are consequences, I just can't understand why they go on and on about it. To be honest it can make my behaviour worse because it gets me so mad."*
>
> Boy with ASC, Year 9

Rewards and sanctions

Rewards and incentives work better than sanctions for students with ASC. For many, their experience of school is very negative. They are often being corrected, told off and are totally unsure of what to do or what is happening. We often take for granted that students will know what equipment to get out, what to do when we say *'Get your books out and turn to page 42'*, or know how to organise and complete a piece of work. All this can be totally confusing for students with ASC.

> *"We use so much implied meaning in our communication that students with ASC are often taking what we say literally and doing EXACTLY what we told them to, then getting told off because that is not what we meant."*
>
> (Jackson, 2002)

This chapter has already mentioned the difficulty students with ASC experience in organising themselves and dealing with homework, teasing and joking that other students are able to cope with more easily. Brown (2015) and Grandin (2014) both mention that an ASC diagnosis is a reason, not an excuse, for poor behaviour and encourage people with ASC to understand that they can learn to communicate their needs and difficulties in appropriate ways, along with learning how to look after themselves and learn and function in a neurotypical world, whilst still being themselves. Rewards that are linked to their interests can be great motivators and with some creative thinking can be built into the student's school day or with liaison with parents. It is important that the school reward systems mean something to students with ASC. The best motivation for a student with ASC is to have a reason to do what they are doing.

School sanction policies can be very rigidly implemented and this may not help students with ASC. The diagnosis of ASC should highlight to the school that the student may need a more flexible approach. We want school to be successful for them and prevent the difficulties students may develop with poor self-esteem and vulnerability to depression. A rapid path to internal or even external exclusions will not help and support the student, even if their behaviour is an action that would have serious consequences for others, such as hitting a teacher or fighting. The next section looks at another way of approaching the more challenging behaviour a student with ASC may display.

> *"I am constantly scared that I might get a sanction point on my card. Every day and every moment I am worried. If I got a sanction, I would feel like I would die. I hate school because I am so terrified of getting into trouble."*
>
> Girl with Asperger's, Year 7

Dealing with challenging behaviour

Behaviour is a challenge to teaching staff when it disrupts the student's or others' learning and work that is given to the student is not completed. It is a challenge when it stops the lesson from flowing or being delivered at all. It is a challenge when the student or others are in danger of harm or accident. It is a challenge when furniture or equipment is in danger of being broken.

It is important to recognise that as a teacher or TA we have an emotional and judgemental response to behaviours. We all have different tolerance levels and different views about what is acceptable or what is not. We can easily react to behaviours that make us angry, frustrated or feel that our authority is threatened. We can easily end up in a power struggle with students as we feel that they are doing things 'on purpose' just to challenge us. Behaviours that are occasional or 'one-offs' we feel we can manage, but behaviours that happen frequently, are repetitive, easily escalate or make every lesson with that student a battleground can very quickly lead to consequences for the student that are serious and detrimental, with punishment rather than support being the focus. Detentions, internal isolation, fixed term or permanent exclusions happen to many students with ASC. What we need to do is implement a strategy across the whole school that is put in place early enough to prevent any of these things happening, and support the student into being able to use appropriate communication and behaviour, however difficult a lesson, relationships or school in general is for them. We need to bear in mind, however, that for a student with ASC, also stopping a behaviour without understanding the reason for it can only cause that behaviour to be replaced by another, often more disruptive behaviour (Moyes, 2013).

ASC behaviour rarely is about challenging the authority of the teacher, however much it may seem initially. Most students with ASC have very logical reasons for their behaviour and it is up to us to try and discover what that may be by looking at the difficulty through their autism perspective. If we take a step back, refuse to take the behaviour personally, then ask *'What is the student communicating through their behaviour?'*, we are beginning to look at it in the most helpful way.

Collecting evidence

It can be difficult to get a wider view of the behaviour without speaking to other staff in the school. Working together with other staff and seeking support will benefit the teacher and the student. A head of year, SENCO or senior leader may take the lead on picking up the fact that a student's behaviour is impacting on theirs or others' learning and take steps to support the student. First, information should be collected about the nature of the behaviour: how and when it is happening and what kind of responses are being used and what effect they are having.

It may be that you need more information about the **function** of the student's behaviour. The logical reasons the student has for their behaviour are usually linked to the student trying to meet a need that they have. What has happened is that they are learning, or have learned, to get this need met in an inappropriate way. This is usually because it seems an effective way to do so for them, or that it isn't effective but they do not know how to successfully get that need met in a different or more appropriate way.

These needs can be grouped into four sections:

> **Get attention** (from adults or peers)
>
> This may be because they are struggling to communicate they can't do something, want to join in but don't know how, need feedback or reassurance, or be communicating that they are very anxious or fearful and unable to tell you what is wrong.

> **Escape or avoid**
>
> This may include others teasing them, noise, smells or other sensory overload, fear of a task or test, being overwhelmed by incidents, emotions or moods that may have nothing to do with your lesson, feeling embarrassed, too many demands, feeling ill, hot or cold, being bored or in their least favourite subject, or overwhelmed by homework.

> **Want**
>
> They may be unable to wait for something and unable to understand they will get a turn. They may be anxious about losing something, or have fixations and obsessive interests.

> **Sensory stimulation**
>
> They may need to fiddle, fidget, stroke, chew, make repetitive noises, hum, self-talk, tap, flick, rock and masturbate.

We can collect information to help us make a good guess as to what needs the behaviour is trying to meet by interviewing the student (**see the student behaviour questionnaire on the CD-ROM**) and by observing them across a number of lessons and out of class situations.

A STAR record form can be used by a TA shadowing the child (preferably without it being too obvious) and noticing the **Situations**, the **Triggers** – that is, the conditions and incidents that happen before the behaviour, the **Actions** of the student and the **Results** of the behaviour – for instance, what the child received from the behaviour. (**See the CD-ROM for a STAR record template.**) This can be a helpful document and, along with the student behaviour questionnaire, can help us gather enough information to support the next step.

What information or skill is the student missing in order to have their need met in an appropriate way? This can be the key that unlocks the barriers the student has to appropriate behaviour, positive relationships and access to learning.

> *We can teach the student how to get their need met in a more successful and appropriate way so that THEY are the one who gains the skills to communicate and problem solve which will support them throughout their adult life.*

> ### Case study
>
> Jack, a boy with ASC, started in Year 7 in a large secondary school after a good transition and was put in a form with two boys who he had been quite friendly with at primary school. In the first few weeks the boys made new friends and drifted away from Jack who was often seen on his own at break and lunchtimes. Jack was quite loud in his lessons, often shouting out answers and arguing with the teacher if he got it wrong, insisting he was right. The other children in his year began to tease him and call him 'Android' as he would get into big arguments about android phones being better than Apple. The more he was goaded, the more insistently he would argue. Teachers were noticing that Jack often forgot his homework, made elaborate excuses and did not turn up when they asked him to see them at the end of a lesson. He became more and more argumentative, threatening to kill other students and refused to work, putting his head on the table for some of his lessons. Staff were reporting him to SLT and were seriously concerned that they could not teach him. Only DT and art lessons were calm as he liked doing practical tasks and enjoyed the designing work they were asked to do. He was imaginative and creative in these lessons, often producing some of the best ideas in the class.
>
> A meeting was called with Jack's parents who informed the school he was being bullied and they didn't think Jack's ASC needs were being met at the school as he never understood his homework and came home every night in such a state that he was beginning to refuse to come to school. As expected, many teachers had reported Jack's behaviour in their classes as a concern, except the DT and art teachers who reported that he was a model student in their lessons.

It would be easy to think that this student is just not coping with secondary school and therefore a different school might be able to meet his needs (and control his behaviour) better. If we are asking the question *'What is the student communicating through their behaviour?'*, even from this snapshot of information we can draw some important clues.

- ▶ Jack has lost his friendships and he is being teased by his classmates, although he is fuelling this through his arguments about phones with them. His parents are reporting this as bullying. It is likely that Jack has poor social communication skills. He relied on his two friends at primary school to support and include him, but they have moved on. Jack is confused and hurt but unable to explain this. Jack does not have the skills to make new friends, so while the rest of his peers are forming groups and getting involved in activity and conversation, he is left out. When he argues about phones he is actually trying to join in, in the only way he knows how. But Jack cannot understand how to repair these relationships and feels frustrated and upset which is exhibiting in his behaviour too.
- ▶ When staff spoke to Jack, he admitted that he found most subjects difficult. He is very talkative and teachers had assumed that he could understand their verbal instructions. Jack actually has slower processing of verbal information, and said his teachers talked too fast for him to keep up. He didn't have the skills to ask for help and also felt embarrassed. Already teased by his classmates, he didn't want to look stupid as well. Most of the time, he had no idea what the homework was, and got really angry at home when his parents asked him about it.

▶ Jack was a student with ASC and for him, if he didn't see the point of something, then he wasn't interested in it. Some lessons, like French and English, were 'boring' to him and he did not want to work because it was meaningless to him. These subjects were the most reliant on verbal listening and processing of language. English work demanded a lot of interpretation and creative writing which Jack found difficult. Therefore, Jack's behaviour was worse in these lessons.

Strategies that helped Jack

Once this information was gathered, the SENCO could see that Jack's behaviour was connected to his ASC and difficulties with communication, social skills and flexible thinking. He was trying to **get attention** (communicate that he was struggling to understand and socially interact with his peers) and he was trying to **escape and avoid** work he saw as meaningless, too difficult and could not understand. Therefore, a support plan was put in place to teach Jack some of the skills he was missing. This included:

1 A weekly social skills group with other students in his year group, focusing on friendship skills, conversation skills and understanding jokes (by student request).

2 All teachers being given a Student Passport about Jack with advice about how to present information to him, ensure he understood and an agreed amount of homework he would attempt to compete each week. This included using writing frames to break down any writing task into manageable chunks.

3 Jack was invited to a homework club at lunchtimes where he found other students working on the same tasks and was happier to get it done so he then didn't have to do it at home.

4 A reward system was set up to encourage Jack to be more willing to try in subjects he didn't like. This took advantage of his special interest, which was animals and art. School put a box of animal books and drawing materials together. Jack could earn time with this activity at lunchtimes or at the end of the day.

5 Jack was also given a role as one of the DT student technicians. A rota meant that one lunchtime each week was spent in the DT labs helping set out, clean and repair DT equipment with the school technician. This also gave him the opportunity to work with other students with similar interests to him.

These five strategies taught Jack some essential skills. He was learning about appropriate communication with his peers, teachers were teaching him how to understand their lessons and giving him more support to do so, and he was getting positive attention from his teachers. Over time, he found some students who liked the things he did and began to form friendships. Jack's behaviour did not transform overnight and he could still refuse and argue if he felt anxious or stressed, but all his teachers were pleased with his increased engagement and willingness to try – even in French and English. His form tutor did some general work about the effects of teasing and name calling, without being specific to the student with ASC, as part of their PSHE lessons. Jack now had the ability to deal with a problem in a more effective way and skills that enabled him to do that more independently.

A whole-school adaptable approach

The difficulty for a student with ASC in a secondary school is that behaviour is often dealt with in a fragmented way. Each subject teacher has their own style and methods for controlling behaviour in their classroom and a student who has challenging behaviours will experience different methods and strategies to get them to behave in each class. The problem for a student with ASC is that consistency is very important. They can easily become more and more stressed because they are in a constant state of high anxiety, and each teacher's different way of dealing with things only adds to their anxiety.

The other difficulty is that no two students with ASC are alike, and each have different manifestations of the strengths and difficulties associated with their condition. Alongside that, they have their different experiences, home lives and personalities. It becomes obvious that a policy that states *This is how we support all our ASC students with their behaviour* is not going to work. The school should have a section in their behaviour policy that mentions ASC and the difficulties that students can have. However, it should be made clear to all staff that each student may need a personalised approach and that existing school processes for dealing with behaviour may need to be adapted. This is where an individual behaviour support plan (BSP) may be used. This can ensure consistency and encourage staff to communicate and work together to support the student throughout the school. A behaviour support planning proforma can be built into the school's policy, prepared in advance and staff training be done to familiarise staff with the process, monitoring and recording. A BSP will need a co-ordinator, a regular meeting of staff that teach or support the student, parental involvement and an interview with the student to allow them to contribute to it and be given the chance to suggest how it might be implemented.

A sample BSP that could be given to all Jack's teachers is included on page 73.

Student: Jack   Form: 7Y

Behaviour support plan

Jack is a student with autism which affects his ability to communicate socially and understand subtle clues, such as body language and intonation. He doesn't usually 'get' jokes and feels that others are always 'getting at him' because he understands what they say very literally. Jack also finds it difficult to understand different points of view, but once something is explained to him he has a good memory and can put it into practice. Jack needs to understand what it is you are asking him to do and will often miss verbal information because it takes him longer to process it. He needs written instructions or visual reminders. He also responds well to pictures, charts and large amounts of text broken into manageable chunks in lessons. Jack loves art, knows a lot about animals and natural history, and has a reward card he will carry with him to each. Please fill this in at the end of each lesson. Make sure the proactive strategies are your main focus.

Behaviours	Preventative strategies	Reactive strategies (use sparingly)
• Calling out, arguing with the teacher	Jack has a visual reminder to put up his hand in class: make sure he has this displayed (on the front of his planner). Explain that this is what you expect. Praise Jack for waiting and answering correctly.	Verbally remind Jack to put his hand up. Remind him to look at his visual but don't embarrass him in front of the whole class.
• Shouting at other students	Check that the other students are not teasing Jack. Sit Jack at the end of a table or row and if doing group work pair him with N. or N. Remember, change and uncertainty make Jack anxious and more likely to shout. Jack is attending a social skills group to practise ways of talking and interacting with others. Praise all students for examples of good interactions, such as listening to what others say, giving compliments and asking good questions.	Verbally ask Jack to speak politely and distract him with praise or attention to his task. If others have goaded him, remind him you will sort it out.
• Talking about animals or Android phones in the middle of lessons	Verbally remind Jack that he has chance to talk about animals or Android phones during his break and reward time.	
• Refusing to work	Write a numbered list of tasks for the lessons on the board and make sure Jack is sitting where he can see it easily. Use frames to set out the work, chunk work by drawing boxes around each section, and indicate how much he has to write by giving a start and end point to fill in his book.	Check you have made the work task clear.
• Not doing homework	Give Jack a printed slip with the homework written on and, if possible, some advice on what you want/how to set it out. If a TA is available, they can write it for him and check he knows what to do. Remind him of homework club and the other support he has.	Jack knows that two missed homeworks mean detention, where he will have to complete the homework.
• Being alone at break times and lunchtimes	If you notice Jack alone, don't assume he wants company – ask him. If he says 'Yes', direct him to classmates or to one of the areas he is allowed to go to.	

Persevere and seek outside support

For most students with ASC, mainstream secondary school is a place where they should be able to learn, have many opportunities and build the skills they need to go on to a successful life and career. It is a reality that for many, however, mainstream schools are terrible places where they feel stressed, bullied, confused and overwhelmed much of the time and this is regularly reported by students and adults with ASC. Where school is successful, students have had teachers that understand their condition, support them to learn in ways that they understand, and recognise that their behaviour is communicating that they are not coping. Secondary schools that adapt the environment, provide safe places and opportunities for students with ASC to pursue and develop their strengths, develop an inclusive ethos, use visual and good communication strategies with students with ASC and their parents, are those that build success in their students and give them the skills to overcome problems and difficulties.

However, some students with ASC have such difficulties and anxieties that they find it almost impossible to cope with even getting to school in the morning. Wherever possible a specialist support teacher should be involved in the support of students with ASC as they start secondary school, but also other outside agencies with ASC knowledge may also need to be bought in. This should be done before a problem gets too big. There are too many students with ASC that are in short-stay or long-term specialist behaviour provision, or even not in education at all, because their needs were not recognised and addressed early enough. Sensory anxiety can be a major factor, along with teasing, bullying and overwhelming demands. These can be overcome in the majority of students whilst making the adaptations in the mainstream setting. Sometimes the environment is just too much for their needs and well-being and a more specialist provision may need to be advised.

CHAPTER 9
Managing emotions

The ability to understand their own and others' emotions is sometimes difficult for people with ASC. (There is a condition called **Alexithymia**, which is when students with ASC cannot recognise or connect to their emotions.) It is a myth, however, that they lack emotion; rather, the difficulty lies in being able to understand and communicate that emotion. Understanding our own emotions involves being able to 'read' our emotional state. We need to recognise thinking patterns, physical signs and the events related to the emotional response. Often our emotions are unexpected and instant: we don't plan to feel sad, or angry or excited. Emotions are responses to:

Incidents
(past, present or future anticipated)

Thoughts
(our perception or opinion about something)

Physical states
(illness, depression, exercise and activity).

Often students with ASC in secondary school display emotions inappropriately. As with all students they are also dealing with the surge of emotional feelings that come along with puberty and this can cause different responses. Some become very angry, challenging or confrontational. Others may be withdrawn and detached from others as the emotions overwhelm them. Stress, anxiety and disorganisation might increase and their interests become even more narrowed. Students with ASC may feel acute embarrassment when in the company of other students they have 'sensory' or 'sexual' feelings for, or they may make inappropriate approaches to them. Some, often girls, feel every bit of emotion around them (hyper empathy) which can cause them to feel overwhelmed, anxious and fearful of being in groups of people. Parents can find their child's emotional outbursts are often uncontrollable and distressing, and begin to think that their child is being bullied or failing at school.

Students with ASC can learn to recognise their emotions and how to communicate to others how they are feeling. They can learn regulation strategies so that they are able to manage their emotions. However, we must be mindful of the difficulties their ASC can cause when presenting this learning to them. Secondary teachers can rely on discussion and verbal instruction which neurotypical teenagers can process. Students with ASC will need a more structured, visual and supported programme.

Difficulties with understanding the meaning of words and phrases, slower processing time, understanding different perspectives and poor understanding of cause and effect or actions and consequences all affect the ability to understand and regulate emotions. The students with ASC may have internal processing difficulties that mean emotions have a different physical reaction for them than is typical.

Emotional literacy

We want to promote emotional well-being in all students. This is often based on positive and rewarding relationships with others. Considering the difficulties a student with ASC may have with negotiating friendships and relationships with their peers, providing an opportunity for them to build positive relationships with a key adult or small team of adults is essential.

Having the words to explain how we feel is important. Knowing that other people will understand us better if we tell them how something makes us feel is also helpful. Knowing that understanding that we have feelings and that they affect the way we think about or act in a situation will help a student with ASC learn to regulate their emotions, seek help when they need it and have positive shared emotional experiences with others. These are good building blocks for peer friendships and adult relationships.

A young person with ASC may experience emotions differently but can still develop an emotional vocabulary that helps them understand themselves and others. A support programme can include:

- **teaching vocabulary.** Begin by exploring what emotion words the students' know. It can be surprising that some know very few and others know many but cannot describe or explain how they feel to others. Spend some time categorising emotion words into four sections and letting the students put the words where they think are best. (**See the CD-ROM for an emotion words chart template.**)

HAPPY	SAD	ANGRY	NERVOUS
Glad	Upset	Annoyed	Worried
Interested	Grieving	Cross	Scared
Pleased	Down	Grumpy	Afraid
Ecstatic	Depressed	Mad	Terrified
Excited	Disappointed	Furious	Confused
Jolly	Hurt	Rage	Unsure
Calm	Distressed	Disgusted	Concerned
Relaxed	Bored	Jealous	Anxious
Amazed		Frustrated	Apprehensive
Obsessed		Irritated	
Surprised			

Fig. 8: An example emotion words chart.

- **exploring physical sensations** and effects of emotions on our bodies. Using a body map, discuss how emotions have effects on our physical bodies and sensations. For example, being nervous can make you feel sick. (**See the CD-ROM for a body-mapping template.**)

- learning **strategies to regulate behaviour** when emotionally aroused. Knowing how to recognise their emotions and regulate their reactions to them takes a lot of support and practice and needs to be a positive, not restrictive, experience for the student. This is when the school can put calming strategies, 'time out' and reward activities in place. Time to discuss incidents with a trusted adult can be very important and a key person in school works best. Putting time aside to teach a student about their emotions can be difficult in a secondary school. It may fall to the learning support department to organise and implement this, or the school may employ an autism specialist teacher to do this work.

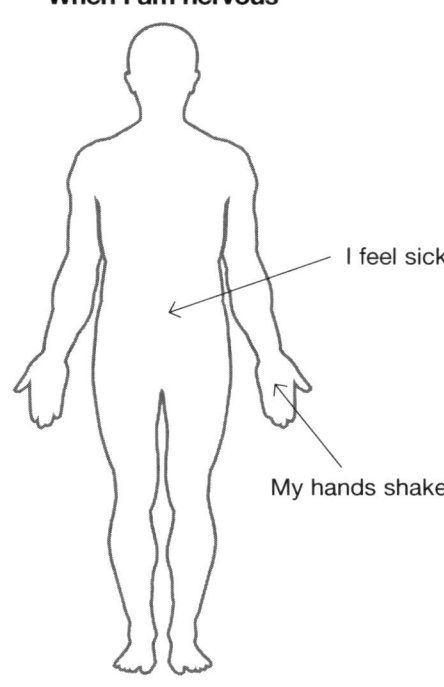

- **learning how to grade emotions.** Use words that have been identified to decide which emotions are stronger than others. A good resource for this is *The Incredible 5-Point Scale*. Below is an example you could use, although students should contribute to their own lists.

Mild	**Medium**	**Strong**
Glad	Happy	**Rage**
Pleased	Cross	**Furious**
Annoyed	Worried	**Obsessed**
Nervous	Sad	**Excited**

- **exploring how emotions make us behave** by mapping out behaviours and thinking about how we were feeling at the time. This includes writing scenarios of situations that are common or have happened to the students and using an emotion map like the one below to discuss the relationship between thoughts, feelings and actions. (**See the CD-ROM for an emotion-mapping template.**)

Event: Forgot homework — **Thoughts**: Will get told off — **Feelings**: Worried — **Actions**: Tell TA

Fig. 9: An example emotion map.

Subject teachers can do a lot to support this work. Emotions do not happen in isolation and so observing and supporting the student in lesson time is also important. One of the best resources that has been designed specifically for ASC students to learn about emotions and how to regulate them is *Emotion Works* by Claire Murray. It particularly helps them identify triggers, body sensations, behaviours, intensity and regulation strategies.

Fig. 10: 'The Component Model of Emotion': a colour-coded model identifying seven aspects of emotional knowledge and competence that work together to show how 'emotion works'. *Emotion Works*

What subject teachers can do

- Know what strategies are being taught to the student.
- Be aware of when the student seems stressed or anxious and notice the early signs of anger or meltdown.
- Be calm and do not respond with your own anger. Know who the student's key worker is and report any incidents and successful strategies to them.
- In subjects such as English, RE, history, etc. encourage student to use emotion words in their writing. Support with visual reminders if necessary.
- Be consistent and support other teachers using the same strategies.

Managing anger

Like all young people, students with ASC are susceptible to angry outbursts and moodiness. Their anger can become a problem when they may seem to be reacting to minor incidents, they regularly challenge authority or are in danger of becoming depressed. Students with ASC are vulnerable to suffering poor mental health in their teenage and early adult years and teachers must be aware of the signs of acute anxiety, anger or depression in their students.

> **Look out for students:**
> - seeming overwhelmed by complex work tasks or classroom environments; refusing to work or comply with instructions
> - withdrawing, challenging, absconding, name calling, complaining unable to cope with other students' imperfections, teasing, insensitive comments or complaining even when not directed at them
> - being bullied outside of the classroom (e.g. on social media)
> - not coping with changes to routines or being obsessive about order
> - not doing homework regularly, forgetting their equipment, being more stressed and disorganised than usual
> - becoming more withdrawn, avoiding peers and trusted adults
> - becoming stressed by a particular issue and pursuing it at every opportunity.

Strategies that can help:

- use a programme to teach emotional awareness and regulation strategies (such as *Emotion Works*)
- identify key adult(s) to support and monitor
- develop good communication and collaboration with parents
- make many opportunities to praise, celebrate and make aspects of school successful for the student
- use a recording system to help student monitor own responses/moods. Let them write their own target.
- use a 5-point scale and inform all teachers of how it is used with the student
- use students' interests to motivate them
- draw out any confusing or misinterpreted situations (*Comic Strip Conversations* by Carol Gray can be a quick and easy support strategy)
- think carefully about your seating plan and have supportive and good role models sat around the student
- make it clear that it is not okay to tease people because of their differences (for all students: race, gender, and disability)
- have a 'Take a break' pass for the student to have cooling down time before anger escalates
- identify the safe, calm place they should go to and for how long
- let the student have a fidget activity – Blu-Tack®, stress ball, fidget toy
- do not take any comments, angry outbursts personally
- clearly and visually remind students of behaviour expectation in your class. Praise/reward (e.g. merits) when they do the right thing.
- communicate with the student and key staff about the difficulties and any successes, however small
- be patient.

It is important that the student is able to explore what makes them angry and how the anger makes them react to those triggers. Using a problem-solving visual can help look at common events and triggers and help the child work out how to react differently. Bear in mind that some students with ASC may find going over incidents that have happened far too stressful so it may be best to begin with more generic scenarios which they can relate to. Once the student is used to doing this you may find that they start to put the strategies in place when they are in real situations and are provoked to feel angry. Being able to 'self-regulate' is one of the most useful skills the student can learn to enable them to grow up and cope in the adult world. However, be prepared to work at this for some time and consistency will be important. All students going through puberty need time to learn to self-regulate and the space to make mistakes and it be okay. (**See the problem-solving map on the CD-ROM.**)

It is important to let the student know that anger is not bad. There are many ways in which anger can be expressed, and some are more effective than others. They need to know that it is right to be angry about some things and being angry is not wrong in itself. Helping them learn to recognise anger and how to express it well can be done with the strategies and resources in this chapter. A good book to use is *The Red Beast: Controlling Anger in Children with Asperger's Syndrome* by K.I. Al-Ghani (2008).

Managing anxiety

There are many situations that can cause anxiety for students with ASC. Individuals with ASC may have more vulnerability to anxiety disorders (Holt et al, 2004). A study by Kim et al (2000) indicates that high-functioning autistic children are at greater risk for anxiety than the general population and a study by Bellini (2004) suggests that adolescents with autism experienced anxiety at a greater level than the general population. Anxiety can often manifest itself in challenging behaviours or obsessive routines and rituals such as might cause an OCD diagnosis. Withdrawing, extreme shyness or avoidance behaviours can also indicate high levels of anxiety.

There are some useful anxiety management resources available to build into programmes of support. Some cognitive behaviour therapy (CBT) programmes have been used successfully with some students with ASC. The principal of thinking different thoughts and taking control of your thoughts can be applied successfully in secondary school. Behaviour approaches such as relaxation and sensory integration therapies can also be helpful.

Social Stories™ can be helpful because they are structured and written in such a way that describes the situation and explains it to help the student understand it from a different perspective. A social story gives them suggestions as to what strategies they can use to help make the situation better.

Often the thing they are anxious about may seem illogical to us but entirely logical to them.

Signs of anxiety include:

- increased 'stimming' behaviours (flapping, rocking, repetitive actions)
- obsessive and ritualistic behaviours, with the student becoming upset if these are interrupted
- wanting to control the behaviour of others, behaviours that demand control
- always tired but not sleeping
- self–harm
- more over-sensitive to sensory stimuli, often distressed
- unusual fears/phobias
- refusing or avoiding places they are usually okay with
- short tempered, rude, answering back often
- excessively pessimistic
- excessive thirst, stomach upsets, frequent requests to go to the toilet
- increased headaches, dizziness
- refusal to work in case they get it wrong, extreme perfectionism
- extreme reaction to criticism in classwork.

Strategies to support an anxious student

- Reintroduce strategies that helped before, such as more structure, visual reminders and timetables and smaller chunks of work.
- Social stories may need to be written with the student to help them understand the situations that they misunderstand or are finding stressful. (These can also be used to remind them of their strengths and achievements to encourage positive thoughts.)
- Use visual signs to examine how events, thoughts, feelings and actions are connected.

- Reduce demands by making timetable adaptations (some students work better if they are on a slightly reduced timetable and space is given at school to catch up on work or do homework).
- Organise a buddy system of other students that might come alongside them and include them in their activities. It would be helpful to tell these students about ASC and help them work out with the student how they could work together.
- Get professional help. An ASC specialist teacher, counsellor or referral to Child and Adolescent Mental Health Services (CAMHS) may be needed.

You can also use the same strategies as for anger regulation which map out the situations and links the student's thoughts, feelings and reactions. Use familiar scenarios that the student may relate to and show how changing what they think can help to change how they feel and therefore how they respond. The *Emotion Works* resource can help enormously with anxiety awareness and management for the student.

Relaxation/sensory calming activities

These are best practised in a one-to-one situation first, to establish which strategies the student is able to use and do actually help them regulate their anxiety. Make sure all staff are aware of the strategies being used and allow them to do them in class. They can be written into a social story for the student to read or have a list in their planner to remind them.

> **Calming strategies include:**
> - slow rhythmical breathing (blow a feather across a table if the student is finding this difficult)
> - thinking about something happy, reading a favourite comic or magazine
> - having a calm, quiet place to sit, next to other calm, quiet students. Consider moving group if the class dynamics are causing anxiety.
> - having a fidget toy or stress ball in their bag or pocket, easily accessible and discrete, (but teachers must allow them to use this in ALL lessons)
> - some physical activity, for example, taking a message to another class, carrying a box to the library, going outside to run in the outside area, stretching and doing wall push ups
> - counting…forwards or backwards, slowly
> - having a trusted adult to talk to and knowing when they are available
> - having a 'Take a break' pass if a few minutes in a designated quiet place will help the student.

Meltdown or shutdown

A meltdown or shutdown is a condition where the student with ASC temporarily loses control due to an overload of **emotion, sensory** or **environmental** factors. It can appear that the student has lost control over a single and specific issue, however this is very rarely the case. It may look like a huge tantrum, with the student causing damage to the environment, hitting out or flailing on the floor. A shutdown, conversely may hardly be noticed in a busy classroom. In both situations the student's brain has been so overwhelmed that it shuts down – a bit like a computer crashing. They often become unresponsive and unable to comply with instructions.

Usually, the problem is the accumulation of stress and anxieties which could have been simmering for some time. Meltdowns and shutdowns can be hard to predict and can happen suddenly, or the student may be simmering towards a meltdown throughout the day. You may not have noticed, however, because the student will be moving around school and the warning signs may be missed or be seen as inconsequential by each teacher. Also there may have been an incident at home, something that did not go the way it was supposed to, or a long-term worry that comes to a head.

Meltdowns and shutdowns are also caused by the effort of trying to cope with changing environments and uncomfortable sensory stimulation, or work demands that they perceive to be unachievable or overwhelming. Meltdowns and shutdowns can often also be caused by overwhelming social demands, where they feel confused and left out, or the student being made to 'join in' a social activity that is too much for them to process. For both boys and girls, hormornal changes may also contribute.

In addition, meltdowns aren't wholly caused by the current scenario, but are usually the result of an overwhelming number of other issues. The one which 'causes' the meltdown is the 'straw that breaks the camel's back'. Unless you're a mind reader, you won't necessarily know what the other factors are, and the student will be unlikely to fully communicate the problem.

> *"I can only describe the meltdown as a red or grey band across my eyes. There is a loss of control and a feeling of being a powerless observer outside the body. I have no control and often don't even remember what I have done afterwards."*
> **Boy with Asperger's, Year 10**

How to help a child in meltdown

Unfortunately, there's not a lot you can do when a meltdown occurs in a student with ASC. The best thing you can do is to train yourself to recognise a meltdown *before* it happens and take steps to avoid it. Strategies to help anger and stress, sensory breaks and adaptations to the school day can all help avoid meltdown situations. It is important that if a meltdown occurs all staff are aware that the student is not doing it 'on purpose' but has lost control and is highly anxious or angry. The priority must be to keep the student and others safe and so, if necessary, safe handling practices must be employed with the sole purpose of removing the student to a safe environment. There should be a core team of staff who know the child well, are trusted by the child, and who know how to calm them down. One of the biggest mistakes teachers make is to crowd in close to the student and talk to them, either in a firm and demanding voice, shouting or using a lot of language. One of the things the ASC brain in meltdown cannot do is process language. Therefore, the most important strategy is TO USE AS LITTLE LANGUAGE AS POSSIBLE. Also, only go near to the student as is necessary to get them to a safe and quiet place, THEN give them time to calm and come down from the meltdown. They will need to be watched and given water or even a covering to wrap themselves in. Often the anger, destruction and meltdown persists because staff try to talk the child down. THIS WILL NOT WORK WITH MOST STUDENTS WITH ASC.

Meltdowns and shutdowns may be avoided if you have warning signs, otherwise you can only try to reduce the stress and effects of the situation. Punishing a student with ASC for a meltdown or shutdown is like punishing someone for swearing when they bang their toe on a cupboard. It won't do any good whatsoever and can only serve to increase the stress, anger and anxiety.

MELTDOWN AND SHUTDOWN STRATEGY		
SAFE	**SILENCE**	**RECOVERY**
Make sure the student is safe and those around them are safe too.	Don't talk unless absolutely necessary. Direct to safe place.	Allow student to spend the time they need to recover in a safe place.

If a student is having regular meltdowns it is a clear indication that they are not coping, they have high levels of stress and further help and support is needed.

> *"I don't remember what happens before my brain shuts down but sometimes I can feel it coming if I'm in a really busy and demanding place for a long time. Sometimes the shutdown doesn't happen until the next day and I just can't focus on anything at all. People have spoken to me and I've just been incapable of responding."*
>
> **Girl with ASC, Year 9**

CHAPTER 10
Sensory regulation

"I feel stress a lot when there is a lot of noise movement or the teacher just changes things for the sake of it, but reading books, having my time out helps me feel better. I can just get away from it all for five minutes and use my breathing exercises to calm down. Then I can usually go back to class. Sometimes I just can't calm myself and need to go to learning support instead. But that's Asperger's for you."

Girl with Asperger's, Year 10

Many students with ASC have difficulty in organising and regulating their sensory systems. All the information we take in from and about the world around us comes in through our senses and dictates how we respond to changes in our own body, the environment, and how we interact or respond to the situations and people we come into contact with.

> You walk into a food technology classroom. You **LOOK** through the door and see the white cupboards and grey surfaces at chest height. You **FEEL** the warmth on your skin from the ovens that have been turned on ready for the lesson. You can **SMELL** the aroma of baked bread that the teacher has prepared. You **HEAR** the stomping of people's feet as the class comes in alongside you. All that information is processed by the brain which then sends you an <u>action message</u> – something like, *'find your seat and get out your cooking ingredients.'*

Our sensory systems take in the sensory information, sends the messages to our brain where it is processed and appropriate messages sent to the body to react. We might do this consciously. For example, a friend phones – you **HEAR** an invitation to a theme park, but rides make you **FEEL** sick, so the action you take is to decline the invitation. Or more often unconsciously, for example, you touch a hot plate and immediately remove your hand away from it.

There are seven sensory systems:

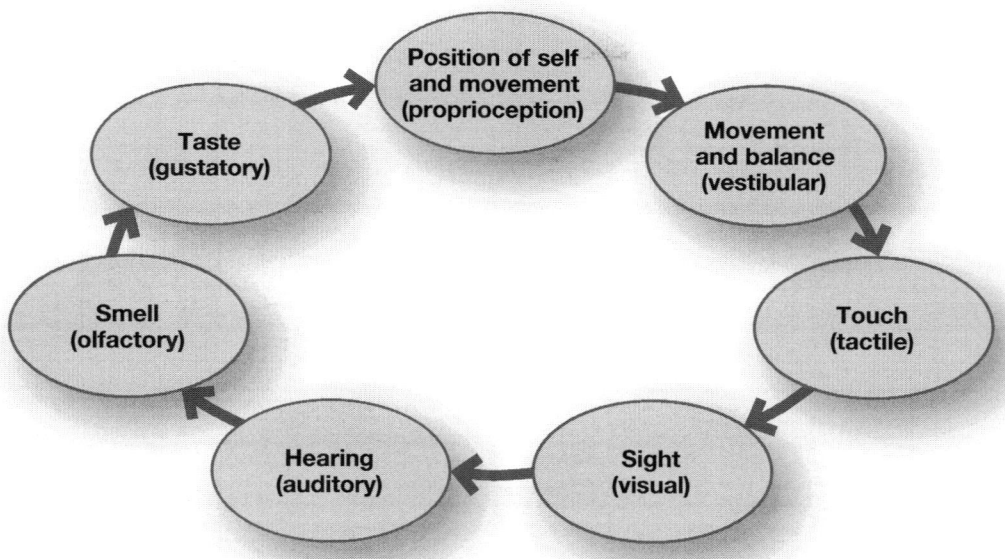

Fig. 11: The sensory systems.

In addition, there is our sense of the state of our internal organs. This involves being able to know if we are ill, where the pain may be, and whether we have stomach or a headache. Some students with ASC, even if they are verbally competent, may struggle with internal awareness, which also affects their understanding of emotions and how they are affected by them.

Many children and adults with ASC are unable to filter and process sensory information efficiently. This can lead to them being **over- (hyper)** sensitive or **under- (hypo)** sensitive to one, more or all of their senses. This makes the world 'too much' or 'not enough' and can lead to the person being affected in one or both of two ways: **avoiding** or **seeking** out sensory experiences to try and regulate the input to their brain.

There can easily be a sensory overload where the brain cannot filter out unnecessary sensory information (think how we do that by not 'hearing' the buzzing of the whiteboard projector on our ceilings most of the time, or the habit of people living next to a railway line not hearing the trains that go by). If the noise, bustle, movement, verbal demands, smells and other sensory information become overwhelming for the student with ASC then they can have a sensory difficulty and be **hyper** or **hypo** sensitive.

Sensory avoiding

Avoiding reactions can include the student putting their hands over their ears, refusing to go into a room, walking a long way round, shouting, screaming, withdrawal, not engaging, or absenteeism. The reasons for sensory-avoiding activity are that the student is experiencing too much sensory input and it gives them pain, distress, anxiety or fear to be in the place where the overload is experienced. They may have strategies to try and **calm** their system which could be rocking, humming, doing repetitive rituals, making noises. This is called **sensory regulation**.

Sensory seeking

Sensory-seeking activity might include a lot of fidgeting, the inability to sit still, chewing, fiddling with a toy or Blu-Tack®, pushing or hitting others, climbing, running and even smelling or licking things.

The reasons for sensory-seeking activity are that the student is trying to alert their system so that they can pay attention and focus better. Not enough of the sensory information their brain needs to make sense of where they are and what they are doing is getting through. This, too, is **sensory regulation**.

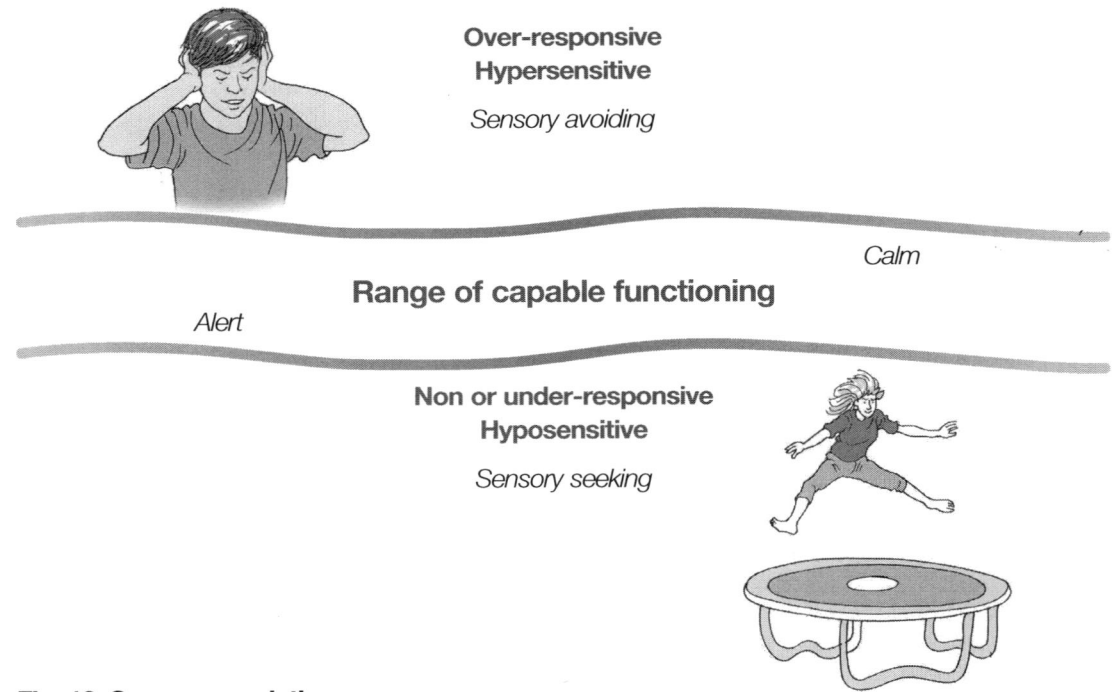

Fig. 12: Sensory regulation.

This diagram shows how, in order to be able to function in lessons, a student with ASC needs to be in their own range of capable functioning, where their sensory system is calm and alert enough to focus, listen, understand and learn. If they are **over-sensitive** they will need strategies to help them **calm** their sensory overload and if they are **under-sensitive** they will need strategies to help them **alert** their sensory system.

Sensory support in the secondary school

Students with ASC often come to secondary school with sensory needs and, although these needs may change, it is unlikely that they will 'grow out of it' and will still need sensory support throughout the secondary years.

> *The difficulty lies in being able to organise this provision within the structure of the secondary school day, but organise this provision you must.*

Each student's needs will be different, but forward planning, outside advice, timetabled activities and working with the student to be flexible and creative can make all the difference. Here are some adaptations that have been made for students:

- allowing them to use a fidget toy or stress ball in class so that they can self-regulate and focus better on the lesson
- providing a Time Out pass for them to be able to go out of class to calm down when they are feeling overwhelmed and before it becomes too much for them
- providing an alternative place to go at break and lunchtimes that is an environment they feel safe and calm in

- a reduced timetable may be needed for some students so that they can have space to do specific sensory activities, particularly physical activities. This can also be used as mentoring time with an adult to go over the school day and review what is going well or not.
- being able to leave school a few minutes earlier than the rest of the school so that they can get to the bus without becoming over-anxious
- any sensory diet that has been put in place by a therapist will need to be fitted into the student's timetable.

For more information about sensory integration, sensory regulation and sensory activities see the book *The Out-of-Sync Child* by Carol Kranowitz (2005).

> *"I work best when the teachers let me use my fidget toy when they are talking. Some teachers take it off me and I think they think I'm just fiddling to annoy them. But I'm not. I hate their lessons, I can't focus and feel really anxious."*
>
> **Boy with ASC, Year 8**

CHAPTER 11
Bullying

"I've seen for myself the devastating impact that bullying has on children with autism. Every child with autism has the right to feel safe and secure at school. We need to act now to make this a reality."
Aynsley-Green (2006)

All teaching staff know that bullying happens in schools. These days it is compounded by online and social media which enlarges the scope of vulnerability to bullying for all students.

"Bancroft 2012 found that unfortunately 63% of young people with autism have been bullied at school. This rises to 75% when we look at secondary school age, and 82% of young people with high functioning autism or Asperger's syndrome. Schools' responses to bullying vary greatly."
Anti-Bullying Alliance (2013)

A student with ASC can be particularly vulnerable to being bullied because they are perceived as being different by other students, are socially immature and can be prone to social misunderstanding. They may have few, if any, real friendships and therefore no one to look out for them or stick up for them.

The teasing and 'banter' that passes between children of this age can be very difficult to interpret and respond to. The speed of exchange can be difficult to follow and formulating a response that will satisfy the recipients is fraught with danger. Not knowing whether to be sarcastic, jokey, rude, ignoring or factual can test many students: when they have ASC, it can be more than overwhelming. If they tend to understand language literally, misinterpretation of the social communication and comments around them can be a daily challenge. They may be easily teased and other students may see them as an easy target. Once the student with ASC reacts in a distressed or angry way to being teased, then it is often the case that certain other students will work out which buttons to press and constantly attack them with what seems to be 'just teasing' relentlessly. This is extremely common and often dismissed by teachers, leading to even greater distress for the student with ASC.

"When girls are annoying they are just a little bit mean, a little bit snide and it goes on and on. Then they act nice afterwards and get away with it. When boys are annoying they are brash, loud and in your face. Girls can upset me a lot more than boys."
Girl with ASC, Year 10

Bullying is a reality for many students with ASC. They can interpret that other students are being friendly when, in fact, they are taking advantage of them.

> *Maïano C et al (2016) found 90% of children with ASC had been bullied compared to 56% of students without ASC.*

Bullying does not only happen in schools. There is little understanding of the mannerisms, social difficulties and behaviours associated with ASC in society and children with ASC can experience bullying into adulthood. The effects of this on mental health and well-being can be long lasting, even into adult life.

> *"Everyone kept saying that '10 plus 9 was 21' and then laughing. It made me really mad because 10 plus 9 is 19 and I had to tell everyone they were wrong and what the right answer was. I couldn't believe how stupid they were. But they kept saying it to me and the laughing was right in my face. I knew they were laughing at me and winding me up but I had no ideas why. It wasn't until my support teacher sat me down and explained that a YouTube video of a boy getting the sum wrong was being turned into a joke, that I realised that they didn't really think it was the right answer. But after that they were always saying things to me and laughing at me. They started saying 'urrrgggh' every time I touched something and saying it was now diseased. I seem to get bullied a lot because I don't get what is a joke and what is true."*
> **Boy with ASC, Year 7**

If a teacher does not understand ASC they may brush off instances of bullying as teasing or banter. Students with ASC who cannot say they are being bullied, who may be displaying challenging or withdrawn behaviours, may not make the connection between the bullying actions and their anxious state. Sometimes teachers believe they bring bullying on themselves as they may act as the boy above did, confronting others with their inaccuracies, telling tales, getting easily upset or being the butt of jokes and not handling teasing and banter. However, teachers need to safeguard these students from being bullied and put policies and practices in place that catch it early on. Other students need to be warned and aware that bullying will not be tolerated and given chance to learn about the differences we all have as part of a wider disability awareness and tolerance programme in the school. The best attitudes are modelled by teachers and senior leaders themselves, and certainly the safest schools are those whose teaching staff all understand what ASC is and how they can support their ASC students.

It is very important that a student with ASC has someone who will monitor their relationships with other students. What can work very well is a regular (such as weekly) one-to-one or small group session where ASC students are encouraged, nurtured and given a variety of opportunities to discuss their interactions with others.

Perceived bullying and hypervigilance

Interpreting others' words, non-verbal communication and behaviour we know is a huge challenge for students with ASC. Some students with ASC may interpret the interactions of others literally and perceive them to have bullying intentions. Some students do not fully understand the concept of accidental or one-off responses that are reactions to events or something said, rather than bullying. It is important to listen to the comments and complaints of the student with ASC. Dismissing them will not deal with the underlying issue. We need to help the student learn to interpret others' behaviour and give them support to do this throughout their years at secondary school. There are some strategies that can help a student with ASC learn to recognise passing incidents as opposed to targeted bullying. These are detailed further in this chapter.

Some students with ASC know that there are rules to follow. The way that they cope with being in a busy, noisy and demanding environment is to bring order and follow rigid rules. This may be the only way they can cope with confusion, stress and sensory overload. The problem is that other students do not rigidly follow the rules. In fact, many teenagers delight in testing, breaking and flouting the rules. A student with ASC may become quite stressed and angry about this and want to tell other students how they should be behaving. Their own behaviour may become very controlling and their complaints about other students extremely frequent. The stress a student with ASC feels about this can lead to aggressive language and behaviours.

Support solutions

"Bullying interventions need to tackle the conversational and social skill difficulties experienced by children with autism (Sterzing et al, 2012) whilst at the same time addressing the higher incidence of bullying that occurs in mainstream schools by 'increasing social integration into protective peer groups' and working with other students towards a higher level of empathy and social skills towards their fellow students with autism."

Anti-bullying Alliance (2013)

Whole-school strategies

- Improve awareness of ASC for all staff in school, from SLT to lunchtime supervisors. Train them specifically about bullying and ASC. Make sure staff take comments, teasing and banter seriously and check that the students with ASC are not being picked on because of their vulnerability to misunderstanding language.
- Have a specific section on students with autism in the schools anti-bullying policy. A good example can be found here: www.anti-bullyingalliance.org.uk/media/7472/overarching-principles-send-and-bullying-school-charter.pdf
- Be aware of high risk areas and times in the school day where students with ASC might be most vulnerable to bullying. Provide alternatives such as quiet areas, school clubs and activities that occupy the students at risk but do not socially isolate them.
- Have a programme of PSHE lessons for all year groups that teaches about different disabilities and promotes tolerance, understanding and active support. Discuss ways in which students with ASC are bullied and how students can look out for it, stick up for them and build friendships. Have a set of 'disability champions' as a student committee and make sure students with additional needs and ASC are on the student council. Make links with a local special school and make mixing positively with students of different needs a normal part of school life.
- Remember that peers can be the greatest support for students with ASC or any special need. A zero tolerance policy of bullying alongside a nurturing, caring and sharing ethos based on all students being aware of others needs and disabilities and how they can support them is what works best.
- Hold assemblies and invite the police into school to talk about disability hate crime.

Student support

- Begin by **making it clear** to the student that **bullying is wrong** and that they should not have to put up with it. They need to know what will be done, when and that school will act to keep them safe. This will usually be best written down in a way that the student can understand. Then do what you have promised to do to make it stop. Don't assume the student with ASC does understand the logical actions and consequences and what will make the bullying go away. Keep parents informed and provide the support the student needs to move on from the bullying. This may involve counselling from someone who is an ASC specialist.

- Set up a **'Circle of Friends'** or buddy system around the student as peer support can be the most effective anti-bullying strategy (see Chapter 6). Include a plan to help the student with ASC travel home safely. This prevents social isolation.

- Teach students with ASC about **managing their emotions** (as in Chapter 9). This needs to be an ongoing support throughout their secondary years. Knowing how to deal with anger, frustration, worry and fear can help a student with ASC have better strategies to cope with teasing and jokes than to react strongly, making them less likely to stand out and be targeted by other students. These are also good life skills and can give the student with ASC the confidence to know that actions towards them may be wrong and they can do something constructive about it.

- **Social Stories™** by Carol Gray, such as in *The New Social Story™ Book*, are one of the most effective support strategies to help students with ASC understand others' behaviour and the situations they find themselves trying to understand. It is recommended that the staff that support the student have some training in how to write them as it is easy to get it wrong, making the social story ineffective. A social story needs to be personal, positive, explain perspectives and aim to help the child interpret social situations. We can give suggestions about how to act or how to deal with a situation and identify where to get help. A social story is not a 'telling off' or an expectation of the child that they 'must' do something differently. The social stories in this book will work best if you personalise them and adapt them to the situation as it is for your student.

- **Draw it out.** Based on *Comic Strip Conversations* by Carol Gray, sit with the student in a quiet place, preferably where no other student can overhear, and draw out what happened – using speech bubbles you can explore who said what, and thinking clouds to explore what or why someone might have done or said what they did. If these are used regularly and the student becomes confident with the format you can also introduce 'feeling circles'. This can help a student with ASC learn to interpret a situation and make a more informed decision about whether it was bullying or not.

- **Worry, Finished, Sorted box.** For students with ASC who worry a lot or who find it difficult to 'let go' of an issue or incident I have found that an actual box in which a written or drawn account of the incident or issues posted can be very useful. Once an incident has been discussed you can decide together whether it has been 'sorted' or needs further action. Writing it down and what action has been taken is very important. Any situation that has been 'sorted'  (use this word – it is very helpful and clear) can be posted into the box. The student then has a physical and visual reference point to help them remember an incident has been dealt with. If an issue keeps coming up, or incidents repeated, it can help identify bullying in its early stages and be dealt with, with evidence already collected from the student with ASC.

- **'What to do if....'** cards can be given to the student (see page 15). They are visual and accessible so that the student does not have to rely on remembering what to do if one of these situations occurs. (We need to remember that memory functions can be very poor for the student with ASC under stress.) These cards can simple state the school's bullying policy and give the student with ASC a way of telling a key adult that will not identify them to the students bullying them. Copies should also be given to parents.

- **Internet safety.** All schools now have lessons about internet safety. It can be very difficult for students with ASC to judge the appropriateness of comments and information that they or others post online. It is common for students with ASC to be very upset by what others may have moved on from, or be very vulnerable to cyber bullying. It is important to ensure that students with ASC do understand how to stay safe online and for this consider materials and resources that are simpler than may usually be used for their age. This works best with the help and co-operation of parents. Use information that is visual and continue to remind them of internet safety often. Work with parents to discuss their vulnerability and be specific and direct in expressing the dangers they may face. Give them two or three options of what to do if they are unsure and discuss issues such as social media and what to write or not, pornography, grooming, lies and even the reliability of Wikipedia, etc. Excellent resources for different levels of understanding can be found at:

  1. www.childnet.com/resources/star-toolkit/
  2. www.kidsmart.org.uk/
  3. www.thinkuknow.co.uk/Teachers/Resources/
  4. www.grannynet.co.uk/wp-content/uploads/2012/10/Learning-Disabilities-Autism-and-Internet-Safety-Parents-Guide.pdf

- Encourage students with ASC to join clubs, know where safe areas are for them at break times, take on responsibilities and jobs (e.g. the school council) and be part of the wider school life.

Communication with parents

It is vital that a good structure of communication is set up with parents at the beginning of secondary school. Parents need a lot of reassurance and more information than parents of neurotypical students.

If they tell you that their child is being bullied, listen to them and respond proactively. Use visual mapping to find out what incidents have happened and how the student is interpreting them. Talk to other staff and students and keep clear records. Expect parents to be emotional and anxious. They know their child has ASC and are vulnerable. It will be easier to tell them if you think it may be perceived bullying rather than actual if you understand the student, their ASC and the situations have been investigated, observed (e.g. someone has observed and monitored break time or lunchtimes). In writing to the parents you can use the social story model: describe what you know the situation to be, factually and objectively. Explain how the student and others may have perceived the situation, without apportioning blame. Set out a plan of action which gives the student some options of how together you can deal with the situations that may arise in the future, how the school will monitor the student and how other students will be supported to avoid situations happening again. Be positive and affirmative. What you write can be used against, or for, you!

Warning: be careful not to place all the emphasis on the student with ASC, even if you have concluded that the situations are not actual bullying. Other students need to learn how to be kind and supportive to students with ASC and the school's plan for this should be communicated to parents too. Remember some parents have ASC too.

Dealing with bullying

If you are monitoring incidents and relationships it should then be easier to pick up actual bullying in its earliest stages. However, life in a secondary school is rarely that straightforward and it is possible that bullying may only come to your attention after it has been going on for some time. The problem can be that typical signs that teachers might look out for may not be obvious, or can easily be missed in students with ASC.

Reading stories or anti-bullying material may help you begin a conversation with the student. If they tell you they are being bullied, listen and act. If you suspect they are being taken advantage of, investigate and ask them about it carefully. Students with ASC can be as concerned about the danger of telling someone they are being bullied. Fear of reprisals, being excluded from social groups, or being seen as a 'snitch' are as real to a student with ASC as any other student.

The danger of teachers thinking that the student with ASC 'invites' bullying is real. Their tone of voice, mannerisms, differences, social ineptness, sensory issues and interests can stand out. Their abruptness and negative responses to interactions can seem to invite regular ridicule and aggressiveness from others.

All schools have comprehensive bullying policies. A student with ASC should not be excluded from receiving full support because they have odd, negative and challenging responses to the bullying behaviour of others. The emphasis should be on ceasing the bullying by other students and giving nurturing support to the student with ASC. This support may need to be intense for a time and a key person may need to be assigned. If not dealt with, the student with ASC can be vulnerable to their education in mainstream secondary school failing. The anxiety, stress and challenging behaviour can escalate to the whole placement breaking down and the student feeling that they have been punished and the bullies are victorious. This really happens, and far too often. Often, without understanding ASC, students can be punished for reacting to others' jibes in inappropriate ways (such as hitting out, escaping from the room, refusing to do something) when that is the only way they can deal with the situation. We are in danger of discrimination if we do not take the student's ASC into account. The Equality and Human Rights Commission (2014) says:

> *"Most discrimination in schools is unintentional and may come about because of rigid policies or practices. Reviewing all practices and policies will help a school to ensure that it does not discriminate... This might mean applying different sanctions, or applying them in a different way, to avoid putting a disabled student at a substantial disadvantage in relation to non-disabled students."*

Deal with bullying quickly and make sure the students involved are worked with. It may be that some time learning about and working with people with different needs may help them become more tolerant and understanding. Class lessons about disability and bullying can be helpful as long as the student with ASC is not singled out. In some cases, the student with ASC has spoken about their autism in their class and it has helped, but this does need careful planning and support. One school instigated a scheme of visits to a local special school to play with the students at lunchtimes. The least tolerant students were changed greatly by the experience and became champions for the rights of students with different needs (see Chapter 6).

> *"There were one or two people but they have stopped now. They were teasing, physical contact sometimes. They were just teasing me, trying to get me into trouble. I tend to know what bullies try to do. They attack and tease you and try to make you to lash out and then go and tell the teacher and try and get me in trouble. My main tactic is just to run. I'm a very fast runner when I feel like it. They mainly pick on me in the outside area and I'd run round the quiet area."*
>
> Ben, 11
>
> www.autism.org.uk/bullyingengland

> *"We moved him at the end of Year 5 because of bullying, which had resulted in physical injury. The bullying in secondary was classified by the staff as 'regular teasing' and was therefore ignored. When he reacted to it, first by school refusal, then by minor acts of violence, then by significant self-harm issues, he was classed as having emotional and behavioural difficulties and excluded."*
>
> Parent
>
> www.autism.org.uk/bullyingengland

When the student with ASC is the bully

It can also happen that it is the child with ASC who is doing the bullying. As with all students, the emphasis should be on ceasing the bullying. With students with ASC it is important to understand their perception of why they are behaving in the way they are. It is by understanding their perception that we will find the most effective approach to ceasing the behaviours.

Students with ASC may:

- copy behaviours seen in others, but do this in inappropriate contexts, and not know when to stop
- make up for poor communication skills by using inappropriate strategies to gain attention, including hitting out, swearing and name calling
- seem to react out of all proportion to any physical or verbal injuries caused by others to them. This may be related to hypersensitivities.

- not understand the perspectives of others and so have little understanding for the effects of their actions on others
- be unable to predict the outcome of their actions and therefore be more likely to repeat them, or know how to change their actions to get a better interaction with others
- have fixations and a way of behaving towards particular people that they find difficult to change.

Dealing with the bullying behaviour of a student with ASC needs to be addressed with the same strategies and understanding as all other issues. Again, visual mapping can be a useful strategy; it gives the student with ASC a visual representation of the people and situations involved and the investigating adult a clue to what questions to ask.

> **Case study**
>
> This strategy was used when a Year 10 student confessed to regularly hurting another boy in his class. Using an A3 piece of paper and different coloured pens he talked about the situations he found himself in with the other boy. **Speech bubbles** were drawn to identify the things the boy said that wound him up and what his typical verbal responses were. **Feeling words** were added to identify when and what made him feel angry and **thought clouds** to try and guess what the other boy might be thinking. The student read a social story about 'what is bullying' and had a moment when he realised that his behaviour to the boy was bullying.
>
> From this a plan was put in place in which he wrote down how things could change. This included him and his form tutor talking with the boy to explain what he had learned. They agreed to start again with their friendship and to learn to apologise to each other when they said something that upset the other. Their friendship continued successfully for the rest of their time in school.

The student with ASC needs to know their actions are wrong and hurt others, whilst at the same time be working with staff or a specialist teacher to learn different ways of interacting with their peers. The most common causes of a student with ASC bullying others are poor social skills, rigid thinking, and misunderstanding of others' behaviour and stress. Exclusion does not deal with these issues or enable the student with ASC to overcome their wrong behaviours.

Help is needed to:

- improve mental health and self-esteem
- change thinking patterns
- know clearly the boundaries for acceptable behaviour (see Chapter 8)
- develop more appropriate social interaction skills (see Chapter 6)
- learn how to solve problems
- redirect energy and the feeling of needing to be in control or have power over others (often linked to high stress and poor self-esteem)
- regulate emotions and know what coping strategies work for them (see Chapter 9).

A student with ASC can be successful at secondary school but they will have greater challenges than most neurotypical students. Supporting their social inclusion will go a long way in helping them succeed, as a group of friends can be the most effective way of being protected from bullying and developing positive self-esteem. It is more than possible for them to have a group of friends that have similar interests, enjoy each others' sense of humour and who keep each other safe when others try to tease or bully them.

CHAPTER 12
Sex and relationships

"Not knowing how to behave or the consequences of sexual activity can leave people with autism vulnerable to getting into trouble, abuse or exploitation. It is vital that they develop the knowledge and skills they need to keep them safe. The support of professionals, parents and carers can be crucial."
National Autistic Society (2014)

Adolescence

Students with ASC go through the same process of puberty as other students. Physically they are changing, hormones surge and strong emotions come and go without warning. Students with ASC all have different responses to their growing up, as all students do, but because they have ASC too, there are additional challenges to overcome.

Typical adolescence	Additional challenges of having ASC
• Physical growth, changes and development of the brain	• Change is often difficult to cope with and can cause high levels of anxiety and stress. Some students with ASC develop maturity much slower than neurotypical students.
• Hormones causing strong emotions and moodiness	• May not understand or be able to interpret emotions. Strength of moods can be extreme. Increased risk of mental health difficulties. Sensory differences and difficulties can ease at this stage or intensify.
• Learning about and developing personal identity. They may try out different personas and identity groups. Establishing their sexual identity takes place over these years.	• Personal identity and group identity can be difficult because of poor social inclusion and interpretation. Some students join rigid groups which have a visual identity. Confusion about identity can continue much longer for students with ASC.
• Relationships with peers begin to take precedence over relationships with parents. They are developing independence and testing boundaries.	• Their vulnerability and immaturity means greater supervision is needed from parents whilst students may want to be more independent and so conflict at home is common. Students with ASC can have difficulty with organisation, planning and looking after themselves which impacts on their ability to be independent.
• Difficulty in looking at circumstances from other points of view. Self-centredness and selfishness are common complaints. They develop more empathy through their teenage years.	• Difficulties with understanding other people's thoughts and feelings, difficulties with 'reading' social situations and having the communication skills to discuss and understand other people's points of view can make people with ASC seem as if they have developed little or no empathy. This is not the case: it is usually the lack of social communication and understanding that means they find it difficult to show empathy.

A sex and relationship (SRE) curriculum for students with ASC

"Sex and relationship education (SRE) is compulsory from age 11 onwards. It involves teaching children about reproduction, sexuality and sexual health. It doesn't promote early sexual activity or any particular sexual orientation.

Some parts of sex and relationship education are compulsory – these are part of the national curriculum for science. Parents can withdraw their children from all other parts of sex and relationship education if they want."

National Curriculum 2014

It is unusual for schools to have a specific section of their SRE policy that covers the approach and support for students with ASC. Students with ASC find SRE lessons difficult for a number of reasons:

- Difficulties with communication mean that they often don't understand. They don't ask for clarification and often misinterpret what has been discussed and taught in these lessons. There is a real danger in taking things literally and acting upon this.
- Difficulties in forming friendships and understanding relationships mean they have less experience to draw upon, find it difficult to approach others in appropriate ways and can be extremely self-conscious or lack awareness of the impact of their interactions have on others, including sexually motivated behaviours.
- They may interpret media representations of relationships behaviour as factual and try to act these scenarios out (YouTube, soaps, adverts, etc.)
- They may not understand language and context and may use sexual language and display sexual behaviours inappropriately at school, at home and online.
- Sensory differences will now include sexual feelings which can lead to strong desires to satisfy these needs. It can also lead to extreme touch-seeking or avoidance.
- They are extremely vulnerable to being taken advantage of by others because they may not fully understand the issues of consent. This vulnerability is the most important issue for students with ASC.
- Some students with ASC have a poor understanding and concept of self and this can make them very easily confused about gender identity, sexual preferences and how to conduct safe relationships.

Safeguarding, consent and healthy relationships

There are some common difficulties that happen in schools that subject teachers need to be aware of and know how to deal with. If teachers are aware, then the student with ASC will receive a consistent response from each teacher and they can avoid the kind of responses that are fuelled by shock, indignation and misinterpretation that only make a situation worse for the student. Students with ASC find it difficult to put boundaries in place and self-check their behaviour as they find it difficult to interpret the responses of others. Alongside that there are so many mixed messages from their peers, the media and society in general that we can help them by teaching them how to develop their own 'moral code' in which they learn to make good choices and have boundaries around sex and relationships that keep them and others safe and show mutual respect. This is an area of the curriculum and supporting the student that ideally should be done in partnership with parents. One way to do this would be to set up a regular parents' group where parents and a member of staff can discuss these and other issues and share ideas and resources.

Sexual language

Students with ASC can use sexual language to get a reaction from their peers (in an attempt to be socially included) or to try and communicate to someone that they like them. Unfortunately this often comes without understanding the context and effect their words have on others. It is a good idea to deal with this early on and use a visual support such as a Social Story™ to teach the student what is appropriate and enable them to put boundaries in place. Class teachers should know what the social story says and when the student says something inappropriate, calmly remind them of it and explain what would be a polite way to speak. This way the student is being taught about respectful language rather than only be told off for using the wrong language.

Touch and personal space

Some students with ASC have heightened touch sensitivity through puberty, making them very anxious and avoid others touching them, whereas others may enjoy and seek out touch. However, teenagers tend to interpret touch as having sexual connotations and, generally, the difference in how males and females display personal space and physical contact is complex and open to many layers of interpretation. We need to support students with ASC in learning about touch and personal space whilst teaching them to interpret others intentions. Using the 'social detective' approach in Chapter 6 can be very useful along with social stories and role-play. It is important to help the student gain the skills to make good guesses and be able to decide if someone's touch is 'safe' for them and that their touch to others must also be 'safe' for the person. Subject teachers can help by understanding that body language, personal space and touch are difficult to work out for students with ASC and explain clearly what you want them to do, instead of the inappropriate behaviour you have seen (e.g. *'Please stand at least one step back from <insert name> so you are not in their personal space.'*).

> *"Actually I have problems with my balance and I hate standing in a space on my own, it makes me feel dizzy. I always stand right next to people and lean on them or the wall. I'm always getting told to stand up straight. Sometimes I get punched by people in the line because I've leaned on them."*
>
> **Boy with Asperger's, Year 8**

You can teach the student about **intimate, personal** and **friendship** space and show this with pictures and practise with role-play. It is important to acknowledge that teenagers don't often stick to the rules and that they will see many instances of the rules being broken. However, explaining that being aware of these things will give them 'social sense' and keep them safe if someone wants to treat them badly or make them do something that is inappropriate or dangerous, will go some way to helping students with ASC stay safe.

A useful resource is the NSPCC's 'Underwear Rule' campaign, which states that any area of the body covered by underwear should not be touched by others or displayed to others.

Consent and vulnerability

Teachers should be aware of, and looking out for, students with ASC as they are very vulnerable to being taken advantage of. They may be 'dared' to do things that others would not do and comply because they want to be popular or do not have the skills to say 'No'. They often believe it as truth when 'everyone's doing it' and seek to be able to boast of their conquests too. The subtle bullying that can happen on social media as well as in school will need to be monitored and dealt with. It is definitely worth considering supporting a student with ASC with a 'buddy system' and teaching peers about ASC so that they can be a peer support rather than ridicule the student because they do not understand. The concept of consent should be explored with the student in a way they can understand and support given to remind them regularly. They should know where to get help and understand that they need to respect '*No*' when someone else says it to them.

> *"I had this social story that said it was okay for people to touch my back and head as long as they asked. So when a girl asked me if she could stroke my hair I said 'Yes' because the story didn't say what to do if I didn't want her to. I hated it."*
> Girl with Asperger's, Year 10

> *"I always sat next to this girl because the teachers thought I was a sensible boy. I knew she was autistic, but I wish they had told me more about it. I ended up getting really annoyed with the way she kept touching me and saying really odd things to me. If I had known, I could have helped her better."*
> Boy without ASC, Year 11

Obsessive interest and activities

Students with ASC can become fixated on a particular person they like or activity that is sexually motivated. This becomes their focus and obsession, with the danger of it impacting greatly on the person they are fixated on. Boys and girls with ASC may follow someone, send them gifts and constantly talk about them. They may have had no response of feedback from the person but they can be convinced the person likes them. Often they have taken advice from social media, peers, PSHE lessons or magazines that say how to get a girl/boyfriend and are interpreting it literally. In some cases the police were called and the student with ASC accused of stalking the person. It is important for a student with ASC who may engage in this behaviour not to be labelled as a stalker, but to be helped to see how their behaviour is impacting on others and what they could do instead. Often, once the situation is explained clearly to the student, they are quite embarrassed and change their behaviour immediately. Again, subject teachers should not react in anger or shock when they see or hear evidence of this behaviour. Instead they should speak to the student to discover what they are doing and why they like the person they are fixated on, and help them to understand what is appropriate and what is not. Their behaviour should also be explained to the person who they are interested in so that they understand that the intention is friendly, not sinister.

Public masturbation can become an obsession for some students, both boys and girls. This should be treated as a sensory issue in most instances and the student given guidance on what times and places are appropriate to engage in this activity. They should also be taught personal hygiene so that they wash their hands after engaging in this activity or any touching of their private parts.

A five-phase approach

> *"Sex education is acquired through a systematic process, just like any other concept or skill. For people with ASC this means a highly structured, individualised way using concrete strategies wherever possible."*
> TEACCH Report (2010)

The TEACCH® Autism programme has suggested a five-phase approach for teaching students with ASC about puberty, sex and relationships. This would work well as a strand of the secondary school

SRE policy and implemented alongside the regular SRE programme for other students. Taking students with ASC out of SRE lessons and providing alternative lessons that are tailored for students with ASC and at a pace they can comprehend can be very successful and give the students the chance to discuss their concerns and ask questions without the fear of being made fun of.

The programme includes teaching:

1 Discrimination skills
- A sense of self and others
- Feelings and emotions
- Understanding the concepts of *public* and *private*
- Differences between self and others, others and others – gender, age, appearance, characteristics, likes and dislikes
- Appropriate social interaction – touch, respect, behaviour, skills, recognising this in others, kindness, public, private

2 Personal hygiene
- Toileting, appropriate places, washing hands
- Cleaning themselves in bath or shower, using deodorant, washing/cutting hair, cleaning teeth
- Changing clothes, getting clothes cleaned
- Food-related hygiene, healthy eating
- Girl's menstrual cycle hygiene; boy's private area hygiene

3 Body parts and their functions
- Limbs and visible features
- Internal organs including sexual organs. Use proper names as well as help students be aware of common and slang terms.
- How the body changes through puberty – including menstruation and how to wear sanitary products for girls
- Feelings and emotions

> *"In providing education about body parts and functions to someone with autism it is extremely important to be very, very explicit and concrete even if it involves using words and terms that you are not normally comfortable with."*
> Lynn Moxon (2012)

4 Relationships
- Friendship, peers, adult roles and responsibilities, wider community
- Stranger and danger awareness
- Feelings and emotions
- Groups, clubs, social life
- Who can they trust, where you can get help
- Decoding others' behaviour ('social detectives', Chapter 6)
- Difference between friends/special relationships, intimacy, respect, etc.

- Appropriate touch, staying safe, respecting others
- Small-talk, conversations, asking someone on a date, etc.
- Understanding, respecting and saying '*No*' (the importance of consent)
- Morals and values held by others

5 Sex education programme
- Deciding whether the student joins in class lessons or has small group sessions with other students with similar difficulties
- Following the school's programme of study but checking understanding for literal interpretation – may need social story explanations breaking the information down into manageable chunks or a different programme of study that is more appropriate for their cognitive level
- Being honest and aware of misinterpretation/literal understanding
- Support to look at the views and opinions and motives of others
- Mapping things out so they can 'see' the connections and consequences
- Supported by specially trained staff where possible
- A clear record of what has been covered and issues raised
- Lots of checking understanding

Cognitive and social development

Students with ASC may be very academically able or have associated learning difficulties. They may have areas of genius or be of average ability. Most students with ASC tend to have a very uneven profile of abilities and development. Their cognitive and social development does not follow the ages and stages of 'typical' students, and they can be developing physically and sexually without having the cognitive and social maturity to fully understand or cope with what is happening. All teenagers continue to develop and mature well into their 20s and 30s, and students with ASC may be some way behind in these areas. In planning a SRE programme this should be taken into account and students who seem young and naïve should have differentiated materials. There are good materials that have been created for young people with learning disabilities and ASC which are visual, clearly explained and more appropriate for these students. (**See below.**)

Autism Independent UK (2015). Sexuality and autism © TEACHH report. autism www.autismuk.com/?page_id=1307

Hartman D (2014). Sexuality and relationships education for children and adolescents with autism spectrum disorders. London. Jessica Kingsley Publishers.

Hartman D (2015a). The growing up book for boys: what boys on the autism spectrum need to know! London. Jessica Kingsley Publishers.

Hartman D (2015b). The growing up book for girls: what girls on the autism spectrum need to know! London. Jessica Kingsley Publishers.

Kelly A (2004). Talkabout relationships. Milton Keynes. Speechmark Publishing.

Kelly A & Sainsbury B (2009). Talkabout for teenagers: developing social and emotional communication skills. Milton Keynes. Speechmark Publishing.

National Autistic Society (2015). Sex education and children and young people with an autism spectrum disorder. www.nasmorayandnairn.org.uk/wp-content/uploads/2014/03/Sex-Ed-and-ASDs.pdf

The Children's Learning Disability Nursing Team (2009). Puberty and sexuality for children and young people with a disability. www.rsehub.org.uk/media/16503/54-Puberty-Sexuality-for-Children-and-Young-People-with-a-learning-disability.pdf

Wrobel M (2003). Taking care of myself: a hygiene, puberty and personal curriculum for young people with autism. Arlington. Future Horizons.

CHAPTER 13
Transitions between Key Stages 3–4 and 4–5

Transitions between schools and key stages can be some of the most difficult times. It can involve disrupted routines, loss of the familiar and difficulty in imagining what the change will be like. It can cause anxiety about different people (staff and students), different environments (sensory issues, where to sit, different uniform, what will be there, dinner canteen, different break times) and difficulty in being able to plan and organise themselves for the change. The step from Key Stage 3 to Key Stage 4 involves transition to new or fewer subjects being studied, but a lot more pressure leading up to exams and making decisions about what to do after GCSEs.

Key Stages 3–4

Students with ASC can have difficulty imaging what an unfamiliar and changing situation might be like and this can lead to stress building up as a time of change and transition approaches. Traditionally, Key Stage 4 begins in Year 10 but recently some schools are bringing this down to Year 9 to be able to cover the demands of the new exam syllabuses. Whether it begins in Year 9 or Year 10, the build-up to Key Stage 4 begins the year before the students need to choose options.

Common issues

- Making choices, often limited options and having to do subjects that they may not enjoy.
- Anxiety about leaving school may begin about this time as teachers talk about the importance of choices for the student's later life and study.
- Anxiety about exams may also begin as GCSEs are discussed and the importance of them is stressed. Students are now given expected grades based on earlier school data. These can be markedly too high or too low for a child with ASC who may have a very uneven profile.
- The student may have a very strong idea what they want to do as an adult (e.g. farmer, games developer, plumber) but may not see how some subjects are relevant to their chosen career, and therefore not want to study them, or they may have no idea what they want to do.
- Students can become fixated on a choice or lack of choice that is unrealistic or unsuitable.
- Students may be quite definite about the subjects they want to study and be very motivated to make the transition to Key Stage 4 because of this.

"I had to do BTEC science and got really upset because I wanted to do triple science. I was so upset I wrote to the governors to sack the headteacher and insisted they change the decision. After a while, my support teacher helped me understand that I could still do what I wanted at college with my BTEC. I was okay, but still upset inside for a long time."

Boy with Asperger's, Year 10

"I was so glad not to have to do some subjects that I found really hard, but I became really worried about GCSEs even before I made my choices. I couldn't choose because I felt so sick and my brain could not think it through. In the end I let my mum choose for me. I trust her."

Boy with ASC, Year 10

What can help?

- Extra time spent with the student to explore their strengths, interests and possible choices that can be made can help, as can mind maps or some kind of visual mapping to show how things link together and what options are available after GCSEs. (**See the transition map on the CD-ROM.**)
- Social Stories™ may help the student understand reasons why and clarify things they misunderstand.
- Above all, extra time to go through and process option information and a meeting with parents is invaluable.

Key Stage 4 to Key Stage 5

"All I could think about was that I would be homeless because I couldn't get a job if I didn't know what I wanted to do and if I didn't work I couldn't afford a house. It made me cry every night and made me cling to my mum. I hadn't done that since I was young."

Boy with Asperger's, Year 10

However difficult or successful it has been, school has usually been a structured constant in the life of a student with ASC. Now the law states that they should stay in education or training until the age of 18 there are many choices available and probably a whole new environment to consider.

The anxiety about this can begin in Year 10, but certainly in Year 11, with the decisions that have to be made on top of exam pressure. There is a wide variety in the help available depending on the student's academic and ASC needs, whether they have an EHC Plan, and the support services in the area. If they are on the SEND register there should be an adviser from the young people's service who will visit the student at school and attend the transition review meeting. Most local authorities have a transition officer to support young people with complex needs.

The choices available to the student with ASC need not be limiting and should include the range of opportunities available to all other students. Time spent helping the student understand their strengths, interests and the opportunities linked to these may need researching, and as secondary teachers may not have the expertise to be aware of all the possibilities, it is recommended to look at this early enough to do the research. Sometime in Year 10 may be a good time to begin and, where possible, develop a conversation that involves parents. College and apprentice open days need to be visited out of school time, prospectuses need to be interpreted and, where possible, meetings with SENCOs will need to be arranged. The 16–19 provision and opportunities differ from place to place. The young person with ASC may need support and reassurance about making new friends, working alongside adults and coping with a new set of expectations which will expect them to have independence and responsibility. There are charities that support young adults with ASC into apprenticeships and employment around the country and it would be worth checking out what is available in your area.

Common issues include:

- poor organisational skills and imagination to understand what leaving school might be like. This, alongside the anxiety about exams, may cause depression, challenging behaviour, refusal to work in some students.
- the student also dealing with puberty and growing up. Relationships are changing and they may be interested in sexual interaction. Wanting adult-type relationships can be very preoccupying and can be motivating or distracting in ASC students as much as other students. Moodiness, anger and anxiety are part of this, and not necessarily the child's ASC difficulties.
- conversely, the student with ASC may be maturing much slower than their peers and may not be developmentally ready for coping with the challenges of leaving school
- often students with ASC are compartmental thinkers and can find it difficult to see the wide picture which is quite important at this age. Therefore, thinking about themselves as adults and all that involves can be difficult and cause anxiety.

The choices at 16–19 are much more varied and the student may have no experience or concept of what it may be like. Therefore, they limit to what they know, which may not be best, or achievable.

"I thought that if I didn't grow up I wouldn't have to leave school."
Boy with ASC, Year 11

What can help?

- **Start early.** In Year 10 have a transition review and make a plan with parents to visit all the options, such as college open days, find out about apprenticeships, etc. Having all the information available means that you can go through it in smaller chunks and give the student time to process what they like and think about each option.
- **Be prepared to be involved.** SEND staff taking students to sixth forms/colleges can make a big difference. Relationships and listening to parents might be difficult for the student so making these visits in school time doesn't impinge on home time.
- **Visually map out the options** – show how the courses or apprenticeships link to what the student is interested in and what advantages there are. You can also add in the responsibilities for the young person, such as getting there on time, handing work in on time, going to college once a week, completing their English and maths to C grade, and so on.

- **Support the student in form filling** (they are less likely than other students to be able to do this independently). Put together a folder for the student with ASC to keep all Key Stage 5 plans together and copy EVERYTHING, so a folder can go home and one can be kept at school.
- **Use a calendar or timeline** to show key decision and action dates and support the student/family to complete these.
- If not done already, consider teaching **key life skills** such as travelling on public transport, using money, banking and other skills that will be useful for the transition. This works well when in partnership with parents but some schools have been able to use their TAs creatively and plan these skills into school time.

"I couldn't wait to leave school because I'd found it so horrendous. All I wanted to do was look after animals so I found a college who did animal care courses. My teachers wanted me to do A levels but I was really happy with my course."

Girl with Asperger's, Year 11

Case Study

A school in the north of England has developed a programme of support for their ASC students that includes a strong link with its local sixth form college. From Year 10, students with ASC and other SEND have the option to go to college one afternoon a week. This is timetabled as one of their options. The college has a mixture of taster courses that it offers to a cluster of schools and offers some students the chance to sit in on lessons that they might be studying in Year 12. The school has incorporated a programme of life skills into this and the students learn how to use public transport, use money and buy their lunch and find their way around the college independently. The students are gaining confidence, being more motivated to work and study for their GCSEs and making informed choices about their future study paths. The college gains students who are comfortable in their environment, have already made friends and whose support needs have already been assessed. This is currently funded by the school who see it as part of their SEND provision.

CHAPTER 14
Conclusion

Autism is a diverse and wide spectrum condition. Students with ASC can have other co-existing conditions and have complex needs. They also go through puberty, grow and change as all students do, and in their time at secondary school will be transformed into a person that will be quite different from the child that you started with in Year 7. The challenge is to prepare them for the next stage in their lives, and the support and additional teaching they need may be different or similar to their peers. How that is co-ordinated and developed cohesively in a secondary school, across a large number of staff and environments is a real challenge. A strong SEND focus in a secondary school and a SENCO who is part of the SLT can help this enormously.

As was said in Chapter 1, ASC affects every student differently and nothing can replace a thorough knowledge of the student – their strengths, interests, personality, talents and difficulties. We must take account of the differences we may see in boys and girls on the spectrum and not make assumptions. It is hoped that this book will provide the SENCO, subject teachers and teaching support staff with an easy reference that will guide them through the secondary school years. SENCOs can use it to guide the long-term support for the student and to monitor that their ASC needs are being met.

A good transition is something that will help a student with ASC settle into the secondary school and deal with the challenges they may face. If all staff who teach Year 7 are trained and given the information they need about students with ASC, a consistent and supportive environment can be developed. Early problems and barriers can be identified and support put in place early enough to help the student. Chapter 2 explores issues surrounding successful transition. Students with ASC can have communication difficulties that impact on their access to learning, both in their understanding of the communication that you, the teacher, present to them and their ability to communicate what they are learning in a way that 'conforms' to the standards of the curriculums we are teaching them. Chapter 3 explores the ways in which learning can be made accessible through good communication practice, including writing challenges and developing group work.

In Chapter 4 there is advice for each subject area. Drawing on the key skills for each subject we consider the possible strengths and difficulties that a student with ASC may have. Subject teachers can focus on the specific challenges of their subject whilst keeping in mind the impact of general strategies that can help the student across the whole of secondary school.

Homework is often a complex issue and for students with ASC a very stressful and demanding task. The organisational demands and anxiety homework causes can have a major impact on the school day. Chapter 5 gives advice about how to support and develop the skills needed to be able to do homework. However, we also caution that sometimes the best advice is to 'back off' and build up other skills before addressing homework.

Social demands are constant in secondary school. The social world of teenagers is often more complex and key to a student's daily experience than anything that a subject teacher teaches them. Students with ASC struggle with social relationships and can be isolated and excluded. Support for their skills and for their peers to come alongside them is very important and can easily be neglected. Chapter 6 explains how social relationships can be supported and developed whilst teaching important skills for life.

Chapter 7 looks at how we support students with ASC through tests and exams, including practical strategies that structure and prepare a student to understand how tests and exams work. We need to understand how communication difficulties can impact on the understanding of exam questions and be aware of what extra teaching may be needed.

Chapter 8 teaches us that behaviour is communication. Behaviour that is challenging for the teacher is often more challenging for the student. To support behaviour there are positive ways of working out what the behaviour means so that we can put in much more effective support to help a student feel safe, supported and able to manage their emotions.

Emotional and sensory regulation is often a challenge for students with ASC; the environment and other people are unpredictable and frustrating. The hormonal and emotional aspects of puberty, difficulties within family and peer relationships can all contribute to poor mental health and behaviour in students with ASC. Chapter 9 looks at how we can support students with ASC in understanding emotional literacy.

Students with ASC in secondary school will still have sensory needs, some of them significant. The school environment is a sensory nightmare for some and for others they struggle to focus and move around in such a large and changing environment. Being aware of the sensory differences and how they impact on the student in your lessons will often be the key to supporting the child in their learning. Chapter 10 gives you some background knowledge and understanding of sensory needs and how to support them in your classroom.

It is important that we recognise the vulnerability of students with ASC to being isolated and bullied at school. There are shocking statistics telling us that students with ASC are more commonly bullied than other children and their vulnerability is heightened by their ASC needs. Chapter 11 helps to examine the issues and looks at how we can support students with ASC to recognise and report bullying, as well as providing links to resources that can be used to help.

Chapter 12 sets out how students with ASC can be supported through puberty, sex and relationships education. With this topic about to become compulsory, schools will need to plan how they support students who will struggle to understand the language and inference and sheer amount of subject matter in a typical SRE lesson. Students with ASC are very vulnerable to sexual exploitation and misunderstanding social cues and this chapter suggests a five-step approach to supporting them in this area.

Finally, we look at transition at the other end of the scale: transition into Key Stage 4 when students need to make decisions about their GCSE choices and, again, at the end of Key Stage 4 when the student is faced with the challenges of facing life beyond school. Chapter 13 sets out advice and timescales for supporting students with ASC through these transitions.

The student is at the centre of everything that is written in this book. They can be supported to understand that having ASC is okay, that they are unique and wonderful and that there will be help and support for them whenever they face a difficult situation. Over the secondary school years the student with ASC can develop and overcome many challenges and when they, their parents, teaching staff and SENCO all work together, then it is likely that this experience can be very successful. We are aiming for a young person to leave school with the confidence and skills to understand their ASC, know their strengths and have a plan for their future that builds upon those strengths.

REFERENCES

Al-Ghani KI (2008). The red beast: controlling anger in children with Asperger's syndrome. London. Jessica Kingsley Publishers.

American Psychiatric Association (2015). Diagnostic and statistical manual of mental disorders (DSM-5™): 5th ed. Arlington, Virginia. American Psychiatric Association.

Anti Bullying Alliance (2013). schoolsnet.derbyshire.gov.uk/site-elements/documents/keeping-children-safe-in-education/anti-bullying/autism-spectrum-disorders-and-bullying-module.pdf - training module on autism and bullying

Attwood T (2000). Should children with autistic spectrum disorders be exempted from doing homework? In *The Morning News*, 12 (2). www.tonyattwood.com.au/index.php?option=com_content&view=article&id=76:should-children-with-autistic-spectrum-disorders-be-exempted-from-doing-homework&Itemid=181

Attwood T (2000). Strategies for improving social integration of children with Asperger's syndrome. In *Autism*, 4: 85-100.

Attwood T (2008). The complete guide to Asperger's syndrome (autism spectrum disorder). Rev ed. London: Jessica Kingsley Publishers.

Attwood T (2012). The pattern of abilities and development of girls with Asperger's syndrome. Archived paper at www.tonyattwood.com.au

Autism, Asperger's Digest Magazine. July-Aug 2007 www.spdparentzone.org/wp-content/uploads/2014/03/Homework-Solutions.pdf

Autism Independent UK (2015). Sexuality and autism TEACCH© report. Kettering. Autism Independent UK. www.autismuk.com/autism/sexuality-and-autism/teacch-report/

Bancroft K, Batten A, Lambert S & Madders T (2012). The way we are: autism in 2012. London. The National Autistic Society.

Bellini S (2004). Social skill deficits and anxiety in high functioning adolescents with autism spectrum disorders. In *Focus on Autism and Other Developmental Disabilities*, 19 (2): 78–86.

Broderick K & Mason-William T (Eds) (2008). Transition toolkit: a framework for managing change and successful transition planning for children and young people with autistic spectrum conditions. Birmingham. BILD.

Brown S (2015). Autism spectrum disorder and de-escalation strategies: a practical guide to positive behaviour interventions for children and young people. London. Jessica Kingsley Publishers.

Buron KD & Curtis M (2012). The incredible 5-point scale. Shawnee Mission, Kansas. AAPC Publishers.

Clements J & Zarkowska E (2000). Behavioural concerns and autistic spectrum disorders: explanations and strategies for change. London. Jessica Kingsley Publishers.

Cumine V, Dunlop J & Stevenson G (2009). Asperger syndrome: a practical guide for teachers. London. Routledge.

Department for Education (2014). The National Curriculum for England and Wales. London. DfE. www.gov.uk/national-curriculum/other-compulsory-subjects

Department for Education & Department for Health (2015). Special educational needs and disability code of practice: 0 to 25 years. London. DfE. www.gov.uk/government/publications/send-code-of-practice-0-to-25

Emotion Works (2016). Welcome to emotion works. www.emotionworks.org.uk

Equality and Human Rights Commission (2014). What equality law means for you as an education provider: schools. www.equalityhumanrights.com/en/publication-download/what-equality-law-means-you-education-provider-schools

Gould J & Ashton-Smith J (May 2011). Missed diagnosis or misdiagnosis? Girls and women on the autism spectrum. In *Good Autism Practice*, 12 (1): 34–41.

Grandin, T & Panek R (2014). The autistic brain. London. Rider Books.

Gray C (1994). Comic strip conversations: illustrated interactions that teach conversation skills to students with autism and related disorders. Arlington, Texas. Future Horizons.

Henderson SE & Green D (2016). Handwriting problems in children with Aspergers. Basingstoke. National

Handwriting Association. www.nha-handwriting.org.uk/publications/articles/handwriting-problems-in-children-with-aspergers

Hoffmann-Zak K (2007). Students with Aperger's syndrome need help and understanding. www.questia.com/magazine/1P3-1388240141/students-with-asperger-s-syndrome-need-help-and-understanding

Hoffmann-Zak K (2016). Understanding students with Asperger's syndrome. In *TEACH Magazine*. Ontario. www.teachmag.com/archives/131

Holt G, Gratsa A, Bouras N, Joyce T, Spiller M & Hardy S (2004). Guide to mental health for families and carers of people with intellectual disabilities. London. Jessica Kingsley Publishers.

Jackson L (2002). Freeks, geeks and Asperger syndrome: a users guide to adolescence. London. Jessica Kingsley Publishers.

Kim JA, Szatmari P, Bryson SE, Streiner DL & Wilson FJ (2000). The prevalence of anxiety and mood problems among children with autism and Asperger syndrome. In *Autism*, 4 (2): 117–132.

Joint Council for Qualifications (2017). Regulations and guidance. www.jcq.org.uk/exams-office/access-arrangements-and-special-consideration/regulations-and-guidance

Jones V (2007). 'I felt like I did something good' – the impact on mainstream students of a peer tutoring programme for children with autism. In *British Journal of Special Education*, 34 (1): 3–9.

Kelly A (1997). Talkabout: a social communication skills package. Milton Keynes. Speechmark Publishing Ltd.

Kranowitz C (2005). The out-of-sync child. New York. Skylight Press/Perigee.

Leicestershire County Council/Autism Outreach Service (2017). A guide for transferring to primary and secondary schools for a child with autism. Leicester. Leicester County Council. https://resources.leicestershire.gov.uk/sites/resource/files/field/pdf/2017/1/19/AOS-Transition.pdf

Maïano C et al (2016). Prevalence of school bullying among youth with autism spectrum disorders: a systematic review and meta-analysis. In *Autism Research*, June, 9 (6): 601–615.

Moxon L (2017) www.autism.org.uk/about/communication/sex-education/top-tips.aspx

Moyes R (2013). Addressing the challenging behaviour of children with high-functioning autism/Asperger syndrome in the classroom. London. Jessica Kingsley Publishers.

Murray C (2016). Emotion works. www.emotionworks.org.uk

National Autism Association (n.d). Autism & safety. www.autismsafety.org/bullying.php

National Autistic Society (2014). Autism and relationships, puberty, sex and sexuality. www.reachaba.co.uk/upload/NAS%20Conference%20Brochure.pdf

National Autistic Society (2017). Social stories and comic strip conversations. www.autism.org.uk/about/strategies/social-stories-comic-strips.aspx

PDA Society (2016). About PDA. www.pdasociety.org.uk/what-is-PDA/about-pda

Priestnall School (2015). School behaviour policy. www.priestnall.stockport.sch.uk/index.phtml?d=162810

Reid B & Batten A (2006). B is for bullied: the experiences of children with autism and their families. London. The National Autistic Society. www.network.autism.org.uk/sites/default/files/ckfinder/files/B_is_for_bullied%5B1%5D.pdf

Sainsbury C (2000). Martian in the playground: understanding the schoolchild with Asperger's syndrome. Bristol. Lucky Duck Publishers.

Schroeder A (1996). Socially speaking. Cambridge. LDA.

Stobart A (n.d). Transition toolkit: helping you support a child through change. London. Autism Education Trust. www.autismeducationtrust.org.uk/resources/transition%20toolkit.aspx

Taubman M, Leaf R & McEachin J (2011). Crafting connections: contemporary applied behavior analysis for enriching the social lives of persons with autism spectrum disorder. New York. DRL Books.

Wertz SR (2012). Improving executive function. www.autism-programs.com/articles-on-autism/improving-executive-function.htm

Wing L & Gould J (1979). Severe impairments of social interaction and associated abnormalities in children: epidemiology and classification. In *Journal of Autism and Developmental Disorders*, 9: 1–29.

Wing L (1981). Sex ratios in early childhood autism and related conditions. In *Psychiatry Research*, 5 (2): 129–37.

World Health Organisation (1993). Classification of mental and behavioural disorders: diagnostic criteria for research (ICD-10). Geneva. World Health Organisation.

World Health Organisation (2016). International statistical classification of diseases and related health problems (ICD-10). 10th ed. Geneva. World Health Organisation.

FURTHER RESOURCES

Buron KD & Curtis M (2012). The incredible 5-point scale. Shawnee Mission, Kansas. AAPC Publishers.

Childnet International (2015). STAR SEN toolkit. www.childnet.com/resources/star-toolkit

Gray C (1994). Comic strip conversations: illustrated interactions that teach conversation skills to students with autism and related disorders. Arlington. Future Horizons.

Gray C (2015). The new social story book™. Arlington. Future Horizons.

Kelly A. The Talkabout series of books. Milton Keynes. Speechmark Publishing.

Murray C (2016). Emotion works. www.emotionworks.org.uk

The National Autistic Society social skills programmes – see www.autism.org.uk

Useful websites

www.anti-bullyingalliance.org.uk

www.autism.org.uk – The National Autistic Society, UK

www.autism.org.uk/about/in-education/bullying/guide-parents.aspx

www.bild.org.uk – The British Institute for Learning Disabilities

www.carolgraysocialstories.com/social-stories – home site of Social Stories™

www.do2learn.com – lots of ideas, social stories and resources to download for free

www.emotionworks.org.uk – resources to support emotional well-being

www.researchautism.net

NOTES